TEACHING READING
with the SOCIAL STUDIES STANDARDS

Elementary Units that Integrate
Great Books, Social Studies,
and the Common Core Standards

Edited by
**Peggy Altoff and
Syd Golston**

NCSS
Bulletin 112

National Council for the Social Studies

8555 Sixteenth Street • Suite 500 • Silver Spring, Maryland 20910

www.**socialstudies**.org

NCSS Board of Directors 2012-2013

Executive Director
Susan Griffin

Director of Publications
Michael Simpson

Editorial staff on this publication
Michael Simpson, Jennifer Bauduy, Steven Lapham

Design/Production
Gene Cowan
Cowan Creative

National Council for the Social Studies is grateful for permission from the following publishers to reproduce images of their book covers on the back cover of this book and on the opening pages of the relevant chapters of this book. Book titles and acknowledgments are listed in order of appearance in Part 2 of this book.

You and Me Together: Moms, Dads, and Kids Around the World. Reprinted with permission of The National Geographic Society.
Make Way for Ducklings by Robert McCloskey, illustrated by Robert McCloskey. Used by permission of Penguin Group (USA) Inc. All rights reserved.
Nina Bonita by Ana Maria Machado, illustrated by Rosana Faría. Copyright © 1994 Ediciones Ekaré, American text copyright © 1996 Kane Miller. Reproduced by arrangement with Kane Miller Books, A Division of EDC Publishing.
Cover from *The Little House* by Virginia Lee Burton. Copyright © 1942 by Virginia Lee Demetrios, renewed 1969 by George Demetrios. Reprinted by permission of Houghton Mifflin Harcourt Publishing Company. All rights reserved.
Show Way by Jacqueline Woodson, illustrated by Hudson Talbott. Used by permission of Penguin Group (USA) Inc. All rights reserved.
The Unbreakable Code by Sara Hoagland Hunter, illustrated by Julia Miner. Reproduced by permission of The Rowman & Littlefield Publishing Group, Lanham, MD.
Sarah, Plain and Tall. Cover image reproduced with permission from HarperCollins Children's Books.

Library of Congress Control Number: 2012949759
ISBN: 978-0-87986-106-3

Printed in the United States of America • First Printing, November 2012

5 4 3 2 1

Table of Contents

Part 1
Meeting The Standards

1 Standards: The Best Place to Start

Peggy Altoff and Syd Golston

The *Common Core State Standards for English Language Arts and Literacy in History/Social Studies, Science, and Technical Subjects* were published in 2010, and by the middle of 2012 had been adopted and embraced by 46 U.S. states and the District of Columbia.[1] They are the result of an initiative led by the National Governors Association Center for Best Practices (NGA Center) and the Council of Chief State School Officers (CCSSO). The standards are, in the words of their opening paragraph, "the culmination of an extended, broad-based effort to fulfill the charge issued by the states…to help ensure that all students are college and career ready in literacy no later than the end of high school."[2]

One of the declared purposes of the Common Core standards is to "lay out a vision of what it means to be a literate person in the 21st century."[3] The document outlines specific standards for reading, writing, speaking, listening, and using language effectively at each grade level from kindergarten through grade 12. Although the main focus of the document is on the English Language Arts (ELA), the authors make clear that English classes are not the sole source of the development of literacy. The authors state explicitly that "the standards specify the literacy skills and understandings required for college and career readiness in multiple disciplines."[4] These include history and other social studies disciplines, as is specifically indicated in the title of the standards: *Common Core State Standards for English Language Arts and Literacy in History/Social Studies, Science and Technical Subjects.*

For social studies teachers, the Common Core standards have important implications. They offer a vision of twenty-first century literacy in which the social studies classroom plays an important role in the development of certain kinds of literacy skills, especially those that require critical reading, the ability to evaluate information, the broadening of worldviews, and the ability to reason and use evidence. The introduction to the standards echoes the traditional emphasis of

social studies education on these skills as essential for responsible and effective participation in a democracy. It points out:

> Students who meet the Standards readily undertake the close, attentive reading that is at the heart of understanding and enjoying complex works of literature. They habitually perform the critical reading necessary to pick carefully through the staggering amount of information available today in print and digitally. They actively seek the wide, deep, and thoughtful engagement with high-quality literary and informational texts that builds knowledge, enlarges experience, and broadens worldviews. They reflexively demonstrate the cogent reasoning and use of evidence that is essential to both private deliberation and responsible citizenship in a democratic republic.[5]

Along with clear guidelines for reading offered at every grade level, the standards recognize that children learn to read through the content they acquire in all aspects of their education. The standards offer specific expectations and suggestions for the teaching of literacy through history and other social studies subjects in the secondary sections of the standards. Although specific expectations and suggestions for literacy in History/Social Studies are not included for grades K-5, it is assumed that history and other social studies subjects will be taught at the elementary level through the thoughtful selection of literature and informational texts by the teacher. At these grade levels, the reading standards identify targets and expectations for literature, informational text, and foundational skills. Standards are also provided for language, writing, speaking, and listening. The reading standards offer exemplars that include stories, poetry, and informational texts, as well as read-aloud texts in kindergarten through grade 3.[6]

The authors of the Common Core standards were well aware that significant content is at the very heart of successful reading instruction in the earlier grades. The days of Dick and Jane are over; we expect that our elementary school children will see much more than the antics of Spot and Puff while they develop their reading skills. Today's educators expect that even the youngest students will learn about the diverse world in which they live—its history, geography, government, and economic realities—while they meet the challenges of becoming fluent and effective readers.

This recognition of the importance of the social studies subjects is a call to action to social studies teachers, and also to curriculum developers and educational administrators in all states and at every level, to ensure that these subjects are an integral part of literacy efforts. At the elementary level, the standards point out that "the K-5 standards include expectations for reading, writing, speaking, listening, and language applicable to a range of subjects, including but not limited to ELA."[7]

In addition to informational texts, the use of children's literature plays an important role in social studies instruction at these grade levels. National Council for the Social Studies (NCSS) has regularly published books, as well as articles and columns in its periodicals, recommending outstanding children's books and offering teaching suggestions to enhance their use in the classroom. Since 1972, NCSS has also published an annual Notable Trade Books list identifying books of outstanding social studies value, both literary and informational, that were published in the previous year.

One objective of our book is to demonstrate to teachers in grades pre-K through 5 how to use literature to teach social studies as they also seek to meet the Common Core standards. This book offers guidelines for meeting the social studies standards as well as the Common Core Reading Standards for Literature in grades K–5 (reproduced on pp. 8–9) as they teach reading at those levels.

In 2010, the same year as the Common Core standards were issued, National Council for the Social Studies published a revised and updated edition of the national social studies standards, titled *National Curriculum Standards for Social Studies: A Framework for Teaching, Learning, and Assessment.*[8] These standards built on the success of the earlier national social studies standards published in 1994 under the title, *Expectations of Excellence: Curriculum Standards for Social Studies.*[9] Both the original and revised versions of the standards were developed for the same reasons: to state clearly what students of social studies should know and be able to do at the elementary, middle and high school grade levels. Both editions serve as a means of broadening the social studies curriculum by emphasizing the "big ideas" conveyed in the themes of social studies, and the concepts and skills essential for preparing students for college, career, and civic life in the twenty-first century.

Both the original and revised standards focus on ten themes of social studies, which "represent a way of categorizing knowledge about the human experience, and…constitute the organizing strands that should thread through a social studies program…"[10] The 2010 edition offers a sharper and more specific focus than the original standards on:

▸ Purposes
▸ Questions for Exploration
▸ Knowledge: what learners need to understand
▸ Processes: what learners will be capable of doing; and
▸ Products: how learners demonstrate understanding

Continued on page 10

The Ten Themes of Social Studies

① CULTURE
The study of culture and cultural diversity

② TIME, CONTINUITY, AND CHANGE
The study of the past and its legacy

③ PEOPLE, PLACES, AND ENVIRONMENTS
The study of people, places, and environments

④ INDIVIDUAL DEVELOPMENT AND IDENTITY
The study of individual development and identity

⑤ INDIVIDUALS, GROUPS, AND INSTITUTIONS
The study of interactions among individuals, groups, and institutions

⑥ POWER, AUTHORITY, AND GOVERNANCE
The study of how people create, interact with, and change structures of power, authority, and governance

⑦ PRODUCTION, DISTRIBUTION, AND CONSUMPTION
The study of how people organize for the production, distribution, and consumption of goods and services

⑧ SCIENCE, TECHNOLOGY, AND SOCIETY
The study of relationships among science, technology, and society

⑨ GLOBAL CONNECTIONS
The study of global connections and interdependence

⑩ CIVIC IDEALS AND PRACTICES
The study of the ideals, principles, and practices of citizenship in a democratic republic

Reading Standards for Literature K-5

KINDERGARTNERS	GRADE 1 STUDENTS	GRADE 2 STUDENTS
KEY IDEAS AND DETAILS		
1. With prompting and support, ask and answer questions about key details in a text.	1. Ask and answer questions about key details in a text.	1. Ask and answer such questions as **who, what, where, when, why,** and **how** to demonstrate understanding of key details in a text.
2. With prompting and support, retell familiar stories, including key details.	2. Retell stories, including key details, and demonstrate understanding of their central message or lesson.	2. Recount stories, including fables and folktales from diverse cultures, and determine their central message, lesson, or moral.
3. With prompting and support, identify characters, settings, and major events in a story.	3. Describe characters, settings, and major events in a story, using key details.	3. Describe how characters in a story respond to major events and challenges.
CRAFT AND STRUCTURE		
4. Ask and answer questions about unknown words in a text.	4. Identify words and phrases in stories or poems that suggest feelings or appeal to the senses.	4. Describe how words and phrases (e.g., regular beats, alliteration, rhymes, repeated lines) supply rhythm and meaning in a story, poem, or song.
5. Recognize common types of texts (e.g., storybooks, poems).	5. Explain major differences between books that tell stories and books that give information, drawing on a wide reading of a range of text types.	5. Describe the overall structure of a story, including describing how the beginning introduces the story and the ending concludes the action.
6. With prompting and support, name the author and illustrator of a story and define the role of each in telling the story.	6. Identify who is telling the story at various points in a text.	6. Acknowledge differences in the points of view of characters, including by speaking in a different voice for each character when reading dialogue aloud.
INTEGRATION OF KNOWLEDGE AND IDEAS		
7. With prompting and support, describe the relationship between illustrations and the story in which they appear (e.g., what moment in a story an illustration depicts).	7. Use illustrations and details in a story to describe its characters, setting, or events.	7. Use information gained from the illustrations and words in a print or digital text to demonstrate understanding of its characters, settings, or plot.
8. (Not applicable to literature)	8. (Not applicable to literature)	8. (Not applicable to literature)
9. With prompting and support, compare and contrast the adventures and experiences of characters in familiar stories.	9. Compare and contrast the adventures and experiences of characters in stories.	9. Compare and contrast two or more versions of the same story (e.g., Cinderella stories) by different authors or from different cultures.
RANGE OF READING AND LEVEL OF TEXT COMPLEXITY		
10. Actively engage in group reading activities with purpose and understanding.	10. With prompting and support, read prose and poetry of appropriate complexity for grade 1.	10. By the end of the year, read and comprehend literature, including stories and poetry, in the grades 2-3 text complexity band proficiently, with scaffolding as needed at the high end of the range.

The following standards offer a focus for instruction each year and help ensure that students gain adequate exposure to a range of texts and tasks. Rigor is also infused through the requirement that students read increasingly complex texts through the grades. *Students advancing through the grades are expected to meet each year's grade-specific standards and retain or further develop skills and understandings mastered in preceding grades.*

GRADE 3 STUDENTS	GRADE 4 STUDENTS	GRADE 5 STUDENTS
1. Ask and answer questions to demonstrate understanding of a text, referring explicitly to the text as the basis for the answers.	1. Refer to details and examples in a text when explaining what the text says explicitly and when drawing inferences from the text.	1. Quote accurately from a text when explaining what the text says explicitly and when drawing inferences from the text.
2. Recount stories, including fables, folktales, and myths from diverse cultures; determine the central message, lesson, or moral and explain how it is conveyed through key details in the text.	2. Determine a theme of a story, drama, or poem from details in the text; summarize the text.	2. Determine a theme of a story, drama, or poem from details in the text, including how characters in a story or drama respond to challenges or how the speaker in a poem reflects upon a topic; summarize the text.
3. Describe characters in a story (e.g., their traits, motivations, or feelings) and explain how their actions contribute to the sequence of events.	3. Describe in depth a character, setting, or event in a story or drama, drawing on specific details in the text (e.g., a character's thoughts, words, or actions).	3. Compare and contrast two or more characters, settings, or events in a story or drama, drawing on specific details in the text (e.g., how characters interact).
4. Determine the meaning of words and phrases as they are used in a text, distinguishing literal from nonliteral language.	4. Determine the meaning of words and phrases as they are used in a text, including those that allude to specific characters found in mythology (e.g., Herculean).	4. Determine the meanings of words and phrases as they are used in a text, including figurative language such as metaphors and similes.
5. Refer to parts of stories, dramas, and poems when writing or speaking about a text, using terms such as chapter, scene, and stanza; describe how each successive part builds on earlier sections.	5. Explain major differences between poems, drama, and prose, and refer to the structural elements of poems (e.g., verse, rhythm, meter) and drama (e.g., casts of characters, settings, descriptions, dialogue, stage directions) when writing or speaking about a text.	5. Explain how a series of chapters, scenes, or stanzas fits together to provide the overall structure of a particular story, drama, or poem.
6. Distinguish their own point of view from that of the narrator or those of the characters.	6. Compare and contrast the point of view from which different stories are narrated, including the difference between first- and third-person narrations.	6. Describe how a narrator's or speaker's point of view influences how events are described.
7. Explain how specific aspects of a text's illustrations contribute to what is conveyed by the words in a story (e.g., create mood, emphasize aspects of a character or setting).	7. Make connections between the text of a story or drama and a visual or oral presentation of the text, identifying where each version reflects specific descriptions and directions in the text.	7. Analyze how visual and multimedia elements contribute to the meaning, tone, or beauty of a text (e.g., graphic novel, multimedia presentation of fiction, folktale, myth, poem).
8. (Not applicable to literature)	8. (Not applicable to literature)	8. (Not applicable to literature)
9. Compare and contrast the themes, settings, and plots of stories written by the same author about the same or similar characters (e.g., in books from a series).	9. Compare and contrast the treatment of similar themes and topics (e.g., opposition of good and evil) and patterns of events (e.g., the quest) in stories, myths, and traditional literature from different cultures.	9. Compare and contrast stories in the same genre (e.g., mysteries and adventure stories) on their approaches to similar themes and topics.
10. By the end of the year, read and comprehend literature, including stories, dramas, and poetry, at the high end of the grades 2-3 text complexity band independently and proficiently.	10. By the end of the year, read and comprehend literature, including stories, dramas, and poetry, in the grades 4-5 text complexity band proficiently, with scaffolding as needed at the high end of the range.	10. By the end of the year, read and comprehend literature, including stories, dramas, and poetry, at the high end of the grades 4-5 text complexity band independently and proficiently.

The revised standards also include:

- Enhancements in the descriptions of the 10 themes and the associated learning expectations
- The addition of new descriptions of standards-based class practices to descriptions of class practices that were included in the original edition of the standards
- A stronger focus on student products and their assessment (www.socialstudies.org/standards)[11]

The 2010 social studies standards present an updated list of essential social studies skills and strategies, including literacy skills. This list, published in the first Appendix of the standards, forms a substantial link between the core reading standards and the social studies curriculum standards, and is an important point of departure for making connections between the two documents.

The literacy skills outlined in the social studies standards in Appendix 1 are:

- Listen, read, write, and speak with comprehension and clarity
- Define and apply discipline-based conceptual vocabulary
- Describe people, places, and events, and the connections between and among them
- Arrange events in chronological sequence
- Differentiate fact from opinion
- Determine an author's purpose
- Determine and analyze similarities and differences
- Analyze cause and effect relationships
- Explore complex patterns, interactions, and relationships
- Differentiate between and among various options
- Develop an ability to use and apply abstract principles
- Explore and/or observe, identify, and analyze how individuals and/or institutions relate to one another
- Locate, analyze, critique, and use appropriate resources and data

- Evaluate sources for validity and credibility and to detect bias, propaganda, and censorship
- Use a wide variety of media to access, analyze, evaluate, and create messages and reports
- Investigate, interpret, and analyze multiple historical and contemporary sources and viewpoints
- Articulate and construct reasoned arguments from diverse perspectives and frames of reference
- Present solutions to problems by analyzing conflicts and evaluating persistent issues.[12]

The social studies standards also identify important research-based literacy strategies that teachers can use to assist students in their comprehension of a variety of written sources. The standards point out that "it is best to teach and practice these while students engage in learning challenging content."[13] These strategies can be divided into three categories: before, during and after reading a text.[14] Chapter 3 of this book includes a detailed presentation of these strategies for developing some key literacy skills. (See pp. 19–28 below.)

Every skill on the list of literacy skills is featured in the processes and products recommended in the social studies standards as well as in the Common Core reading standards (though not all are located in the K-5 reading standards). One example, at this point, will illustrate the correlation:

Social Studies Literacy Skill: Describe people, places, and events and the connections between and among them.[15]

Social Studies Standards
Theme ❸ PEOPLE, PLACES AND ENVIRONMENTS
Knowledge: "...the study of location, place, and the interactions of people with their surroundings."

Processes: "Investigate relationships among people, places, and environments..." [16]

Common Core Reading Standards

Reading Standards for Literature K-5
The expectations for "Key Ideas and Details" show a progression from grade K through grade 5, describing characters, settings and events in stories at increasing levels of complexity.[17]

On a wider scale, perhaps the greatest connection between the Common Core standards and the national social studies standards is the importance that they place on students developing the skills needed to think critically and creatively in order to be prepared for the rigors of college, the workplace, and their roles as citizens in the twenty-first century. While the core reading standards lay out a vision of what it means to be a literate person in the twenty-first century, they also emphasize skills in the evaluation of evidence and in reasoning that are "essential to both private deliberation and responsible citizenship in a democratic republic."[18] A primary aim of social studies, as expressed in the national social studies standards, "is the promotion of civic competence—the knowledge, intellectual processes, and democratic dispositions required of students to be active and engaged participants in public life."[19] In order to accomplish this goal, students must gain knowledge through reading, and determine the accuracy, clarity, reliability, relevance, and importance of what they read. Both sets of standards acknowledge the role of modern technology in acquiring, analyzing and synthesizing information.

Here is another example that illustrates the correlation between the sets of standards:

Social Studies Critical Thinking Skill:
Evaluate Information

Social Studies Standards:
Theme ⑩ CIVIC IDEALS AND PRACTICES
Knowledge: "Key practices in a democratic society include civic participation based on studying community issues."
Processes: "Evaluate positions about an issue based on evidence and arguments provided…"[20]

Common Core Reading Standards:

Reading Standards for Informational Text
The expectations for the "Integration of Knowledge and Ideas" show a progression from grade K through grade 5 involving the use of reasoning and evidence to support points in a text, at increasing levels of complexity.[21]

Increasing levels of complexity and rigor are part of both sets of standards. The Common Core Reading Standards highlight "sample performance tasks." The National Curriculum Standards for Social Studies present performance-based "products" and "snapshots of practice" that are numerous and well described and developed.

While there are similarities in the objectives and purposes of both sets of standards, there are differences in their organizational structure. The Common Core ELA Reading Standards are arranged by grade level for grades K–8, and by grade bands (9–10 and 11–12) for high school. The curriculum standards for social studies are organized by three grade bands, for elementary, middle and high school grades. There are also differences between NCSS and the core reading standards in the definition of "literature." The Common Core reading standards distinguish between "literature" (stories, dramas, poetry) and "informational text" (literary non-fiction and historical, scientific, and technical texts).[22] Some attractive non-fiction publications for children would, however, be considered literature by NCSS; in this book, each of the chapters focuses in depth on a selected work of children's literature, and one of these seven books (in Chapter 5 for pre-kindergarten/kindergarten) is considered literature according to NCSS criteria, though it would be treated as "informational" according to the Common Core Reading Standards. The six remaining books reviewed in depth in chapters 6–11 would be considered "literature" by both.

Ideally, two or more teachers at the same grade level would become familiar with both sets of standards—in addition to their designated curriculum—by examining the grade level and grade band standards and expectations, and then discussing ways to combine portions of the documents to craft meaningful instructional strategies and tasks. The result would be to enhance their students' skills in English Language Arts as well as in social studies. Realistically, elementary teachers seldom have the luxury of extended periods of time to engage in the study required to address all standards related to English Language Arts and social studies. We hope that this book will offer a shortcut that enables teachers to make authentic and valuable connections between the two sets of standards. Increasing students' understanding of concepts and their ability to apply skills can put them well on their way to being fully prepared for college, career and civic life.

This book presents extensive tools to "bridge the gap" between the Common Core Reading Standards for Literature and key content in the social studies, as presented in the NCSS *National Curriculum Standards for Social Studies.* The book presents particular forms of content for young learners, and it gives examples of how teachers should teach to achieve both reading and social studies standards.

The teacher who uses this book can turn to her or his grade level and view a unit using one great children's book that features one or more of the Ten Themes of Social Studies, accompanied by reading strategies that teach to the Common Core Reading Standards for Literature in grades K–5, as well as strategies related to other ELA standards in cases where the book is especially useful for accomplishing these. At the end of every chapter, nine other great books are annotated; these are classic books that address the nine themes of social studies other than the principal theme addressed by the featured book. At the end of this volume is a bibliography of children's books related to the themes of the standards that bring young learners to social science topics in grade appropriate ways.

Teaching Reading with the Social Studies Standards provides an extensive constellation of resources for classrooms from pre-K to grade 5. It provides hundreds more suggestions of suitable social studies books than can be found in the Common Core Standards, and offers exceptional range and quality. Most importantly, this volume was written by social studies experts and classroom teachers of excellence who support the goals of social studies instruction in full partnership with the reading objectives teachers address every day.

The Common Core Reading Standards for Literature are referenced frequently throughout the chapters, along with references to other Common Core Standards (such as Informational Text, Foundational Skills, Language, and Writing), in cases where the book discussed is especially well suited to implementation of those standards. At the end of chapters 5–11, there are also citations of another set of national English Language Arts standards published in 1996 by the International Reading Association (IRA) and National Council of Teachers of English (NCTE).[23]

Most critically, the Common Core ELA Standards are combined in this book with the NCSS standards and expectations, so that learning to read is integral to learning to think about the complex world in which the child of the twenty-first century lives. What could be more important, or more natural for curriculum and instructional planning? We hope that the following chapters will inspire more meaningful reading and social studies instruction in the classrooms of our youngest learners. 🔖

NOTES

1. See www.corestandards.org. A tally of the number of states to have accepted the Common Core standards is kept at www.corestandards.org/in-the-states. As of September 15, 2012, 45 states and the District of Columbia had adopted the Common Core standards for both English Language Arts and Math. Minnesota had accepted the ELA standards but not the Math standards. The states that had not accepted the Common Core standards were Alaska, Nebraska, Texas and Virginia.

2. National Governors Association Center for Best Practices and Council of Chief State School Officers, *Common Core State Standards for English Language Arts and Literacy in History/Social Studies, Science, and Technical Subjects* (Washington, D.C.: National Governors Association Center for Best Practices and Council of Chief State School Officers, 2010), 3. Support for the Common State Standards Initiative of the National Governors Association (NGA) and Council of Chief State School Officers (CSSSO) was provided by prominent education, business, and

state leaders' organizations. The single most important source of information regarding this set of standards is the website, www.corestandards.org.

3. *Ibid.*, 3.

4. *Ibid.*

5. *Ibid.*

6. Appendix B (pages 1-76) of the Common Core standards has been widely regarded as important to social studies as well. Entitled *Text Exemplars and Sample Performance Tasks*, the appendix provides text samples that "serve to exemplify the level of complexity and quality that the Standards require all students in a given grade band to engage with." The selections are intended to guide educators in choosing others of similar complexity, quality and range. K–5 exemplars are separated into stories, poetry, and informational texts (as well as read-aloud texts in kindergarten through grade 3). The document specifically states that these "do not represent a partial or complete reading list." Unfortunately, for some states and districts, this is exactly what they have become. Chapters 5 through 11 of the present book fill a gap by offering the literature of "similar complexity, quality and range" that is required for the implementation of the common core standards.

7. *Common Core State Standards for English Language Arts and Literacy in History/Social Studies...*, 5.

8. National Council for the Social Studies (NCSS), *National Curriculum Standards for Social Studies: A Framework for Teaching, Learning, and Assessment* (Silver Spring, MD: NCSS, 2010).

9. National Council for the Social Studies (NCSS), *Expectations of Excellence: Curriculum Standards for Social Studies* (Washington, DC: NCSS, 1994). The original NCSS effort to develop and publish standards paralleled that of other content areas during the 1990s, largely as the result of the "Goals 2000: Educate America Act" passed by Congress and signed into law by President George Herbert Walker Bush. While social studies was excluded from that legislation, NCSS seized the opportunity to add social studies to the national agenda and named a task force to craft the standards, review drafts, consider feedback from review panels, and revise and prepare the final version, which was then approved by the NCSS Board of Directors and published. The social studies standards have been widely used by educators in this and other nations when planning curriculum for early, middle, and high school grades.

10. NCSS, *National Curriculum Standards for Social Studies*, 3.

11. A description of the purposes of the standards, as well as the volume's opening chapters, and resources for using the standards are available at www.socialstudies.org/standards. We recommend, however, that teachers obtain the entire publication in order to benefit from its guidelines.

12. NCSS, *National Curriculum Standards for Social Studies*, 163.

13. *Ibid.*, 165.

14. *Ibid.*

15. *Ibid.*, 163.

16. *Ibid.*, 35, 36.

17. Readers can identify this progression by examining *Common Core State Standards for English Language Arts and Literacy in History/Social Studies...*, 11-12. The standards are also reproduced on pp. 8–9 of this book.

18. *Ibid.*, 3.

19. NCSS, *National Curriculum Standards for Social Studies*, 3.

20. *Ibid.*, 63-64.

21. Readers can identify this progression by examining *Common Core State Standards for English Language Arts and Literacy in History/Social Studies...*, 13-14.

22. *Ibid.*, 31.

23. International Reading Association (IRA) and National Council of Teachers of English (NCTE), *Standards for the English Language Arts* (Newark, DE and Urbana, IL: IRA and NCTE, 1996).

2 Selecting Literature for Social Studies Instruction

Peggy Altoff

Books that we read when we were young remain with us in special and enduring ways. Many of us have fond memories of the books that interested and enchanted us in grade school. Good books that engage students lie at the heart of curriculum planning for the elementary school teacher, whether they are works of literature or informational text. One of the most important roles of teachers is to provide these valuable reading experiences to our young learners. The main reason is not that our students will score better on reading tests (though that will be the case) but, much more important, that they will cherish reading and see it as a valuable part of the life of the mind that begins for us as children and extends into the civic life of adulthood.

Elementary teachers know the value of reading, writing and thinking in planning daily classroom instruction. They also know that they can enhance the knowledge and skills of their students through social studies content organized in a meaningful curriculum. Good social studies content has become even more essential in this era of testing. As documented by researchers, students "who score well on reading tests have knowledge about a wide range of things... so that whatever they are asked to read about on the test, they likely know something about it."[1]

Unfortunately, the marginalization of social studies since the implementation of the No Child Left Behind (NCLB) legislation in the first decade of the 21st century has jeopardized the ability of teachers to use social studies content to promote literacy.[2] However, dedicated teachers—those willing to assume the "shared responsibility" for "interdisciplinary teaching" called for in the Common Core English Language Arts Standards[3]—seek multiple ways to teach literacy while addressing social studies content. This book focuses on using literature that addresses social studies standards in meaningful ways that

also help teachers to meet the Common Core Reading Standards for Literature. The chapters that follow recommend both familiar and unfamiliar books and exemplary strategies for different grade levels, and meet the call of the reading standards to find texts of "complexity, quality and range."

The integration of reading and social studies can be a complex process, which requires teachers to know their curriculum before choosing a grade-appropriate book. Teachers need to be sure that there is a substantive connection between the social studies content of the book and the reading skills associated with it. Janet Alleman and Jere Brophy offer excellent advice on successful integration:

> To be really successful with integration, teachers need to have a comprehensive picture of what the grade level curriculum entails, including the goals, major understandings, and skills for each subject area, and the expectations for students in the previous grade. They also need to avoid teaching new procedural skills and propositional content knowledge concurrently. As a general rule, use familiar content when

teaching a new skill and develop new content using already fluent skills, to avoid confusion that develops when there are competing goals.[4]

This chapter offers guidelines for the selection of books with the right content, and the next chapter will show teachers how to use literature to develop vital skills among their students. The subsequent chapters show how seven masterworks for children can provide inspiration for mini-units that help children to learn to read while they learn social studies in a well-planned curriculum. In addition to the main featured book in each of chapters 5–11, our contributors will also recommend scores of other books that can fulfill this objective. While the recommended class activities in each chapter focus on a specific book, it should not be difficult for teachers who employ these activities to use the underlying methods to develop comparable activities for other books that advance student abilities in reading and social studies.

A key question facing teachers is how to choose the right books. The initial answer to this question is often to choose what is available or to choose the books that we like the best! However, these choices may not always *be* the best. A teacher should begin by considering the standards that must be addressed, and should select books on the basis of the curriculum objectives for the grade level.

At the elementary level, there are many different kinds of books that can be used to teach social studies. One list that is still useful was published in an article in *Social Studies and the Young Learner* in 1995.[5]
- ▸ Historical fiction
- ▸ Contemporary realistic fiction
- ▸ Folklore
- ▸ Biography
- ▸ Information text
- ▸ Poetry
- ▸ Songbooks

Consider why you might want to use any of the books included in this volume. Each kind of book offers different possibilities. Works of fiction can transport learners to other cultures, places, and times in ways that are different than in a textbook. They can present learners with different perspectives and emotions never before experienced. Dynamic descriptions can help students visualize the actual details of an event's setting. People's lives can be portrayed in great specificity, going beyond the bare facts often found in informational text. In addition, young learners can often identify with the people described, comparing their experiences to personal ones.

As teachers search for appropriate trade books, they should be mindful of the possible drawbacks of some books. Information related to other cultures, places, and times can be stereotypical if the author's research is incomplete or inaccurate: for example, if an author chooses to describe a desert as always hot, dry and lacking life. Descriptions that help students visualize details of an event's setting may not be accurate. In addition, the different perspectives and emotions expressed in some books can be disturbing to some students, particularly if a tragedy is described in ways that are similar to a personal experience. The differences between fact and fiction are not always apparent and must be emphasized repeatedly. It is also important that teachers never assume that students will achieve a social studies objective merely by reading what is assigned; for example, if learners read *If You Were There In 1492*,[6] they would learn about everyday life at the time of Christopher Columbus, but they should compare this book to an informational text for accuracy and a more complete understanding of the people and events involved.

It is important for teachers to be sure that they and their school libraries have access to the best books for teaching social studies. It is not difficult to identify these books. National Council for the Social Studies (NCSS) has published a number of books on the use of children's literature in the classroom and regularly covers the topic in columns and articles in its periodicals, *Social Education* and *Social Studies and the Young Learner*. Since 1972, NCSS and the Children's Book Council have collaborated in making an annual selection of the best recently published social studies trade books, the Notable Social Studies Trade Books for Young People. This list is published annually in *Social Education*, and includes annotations of the books that identify the themes of the national social studies standards that each book promotes. Past lists are available on the NCSS website at socialstudies .org/notable. In addition, the NCSS Carter G. Woodson Book Award is bestowed annually for the most distinguished social science books appropriate for young readers that depict ethnicity in the United States. A list of winners and entries can be found at socialstudies.org/awards/woodson.

A large number of valuable books are available for teaching social studies themes. The selection of books should always be rooted in the standards that must be addressed. In addition to state standards, elementary teachers should seek to select books that can accomplish learning expectations based on the national social studies standards. They should examine the Purposes, Questions for Exploration, Knowledge, Processes, and Products outlined in the standards for each social studies theme for their level.[7] In particular, we recommend that elementary teachers consider the "Questions for Exploration" in the social studies standards document as they choose literature that will help them teach to the standards in their classroom.

As an example of this approach, we will identify some suitable questions for five themes of the national social studies standards. While the NCSS standards address Ten Themes and all of them are ideally included in a comprehensive school social studies program, some get more attention than others in the typical elementary social studies curriculum. These are:

❶ CULTURE;
❷ TIME, CONTINUITY, AND CHANGE;
❸ PEOPLE, PLACES, AND ENVIRONMENTS;
❻ POWER, AUTHORITY, AND GOVERNANCE; and
❼ PRODUCTION, DISTRIBUTION, AND CONSUMPTION.

In state standards, these are often labeled as Culture, History, Geography, Civics, and Economics respectively. Information about all ten themes can be found at socialstudies.org/standards.

The following are suitable questions for teachers to ask as they search for appropriate reading materials. Some of the questions are taken directly from the revised social studies standards of 2010.

Questions to ask as you search for appropriate reading materials

❶ CULTURE
▶ What are the common beliefs, values and behaviors of the culture described?
▶ How are groups of people alike and different?
▶ How do cultures change over time?
▶ How does culture unify a group of people?
▶ How is cultural diversity portrayed within and across cultures?

❷ TIME CONTINUITY AND CHANGE
▶ What events are described?
▶ Are these events described chronologically?
▶ What caused the events? What were the results?
▶ What connections are there between these events and current events?
▶ How are the ideas and events depicted similar to and different from those of people today?

❸ PEOPLE, PLACES, AND ENVIRONMENTS
▶ What physical and geographic characteristics or features are described?
▶ What locations are described? Are they described in absolute or relative terms?
▶ Are accounts included of how people changed the environment?
▶ Are accounts included of how changes in the environment affect peoples lives?
▶ How are regions of a state/country/continent defined/described?
▶ Are accounts included of people moving and why they move?

❻ POWER, AUTHORITY, AND GOVERNANCE
▶ How are power and authority defined?
▶ Are accounts included of how power is gained or lost?

- Are powers or functions of local, state, national or international governments described?
- How are people shown—as concerned/active citizens or not?
- What kinds of decisions do people make?
- What rights and/or responsibilities do people have?

❼ PRODUCTION, DISTRIBUTION, AND CONSUMPTION

- Do people get everything that they want? Why?
- How do people make choices about scarce resources?
- Are accounts included of how goods are made, delivered, sold, and/or used?
- How does the availability of resources influence decisions?
- What economic successes or failures are included?

The above questions are few in number, and they should not be considered exhaustive, but teachers will find them a useful guide when evaluating books to determine the best ways of developing students' knowledge and understanding of Culture, History, Geography, Civics, and Economics. In the social studies standards, teachers can find comparable questions for the other five themes of the standards:

❹ INDIVIDUAL DEVELOPMENT AND IDENTITY
❺ INDIVIDUALS, GROUPS, AND INSTITUTIONS
❽ SCIENCE, TECHNOLOGY, AND SOCIETY
❾ GLOBAL CONNECTIONS; and
❿ CIVIC IDEALS AND PRACTICES.

Books that address questions such as these will give elementary students an important basic grounding in key social studies subjects that will prepare them well for more advanced study in middle school. Teachers who use curriculum standards as the basis for their selection of books have a solid foundation that will enable them to accomplish excellent results. 🖹

NOTES

1. See the post by Daniel T. Willingham, "Willingham: Reading Is Not a Skill—And Why This Is a Problem for the Draft National Standards," September 28, 2009 at http://voices.washingtonpost.com/answer-sheet/daniel-willingham/willingham-reading-is-not-a-sk.html.

2. According to a report by the Center on Education Policy, since the enactment of the No Child Left Behind federal education policy, 44 percent of districts surveyed have reduced time for social studies. That percentage rose to 51 percent in districts with "failing schools." (See Jennifer McMurren, *Choices, Changes, and Challenges: Curriculum and Instruction in the NCLB Era* [Washington, D.C.: Center on Education Policy, 2007], 1, 7). In a task force report prepared by the Maryland State Department of Education, 88% of elementary teachers surveyed stated that "social studies is not a priority in their school." (Maryland State Department of Education. *Task Force Report on Social Studies Education in Maryland: The Challenge and the Imperative, 2010*.) Colorado respondents to a national study reported that classroom time for social studies has decreased 64%. (Rebecca Theobald and Chris Elnicki, "National Study on the State of Social Studies Teachers: Colorado and the United States Selected Measures Compared," unpublished results presented at Colorado Social Studies Supervisors and Friends Group Meeting, Denver, Colorado, May 16, 2012.) Similar statistics have been reported in other states, especially those in which there is no assessment for accountability in social studies content and skills.

3. National Governors Association Center for Best Practices and Council of Chief State School Officers, *Common Core State Standards for English Language Arts and Literacy in History/Social Studies, Science, and Technical Subjects* (Washington, D.C.: National Governors Association Center for Best Practices and Council of Chief State School Officers, 2010), 4.

4. Janet Alleman and Jere Brophy, "Effective Integration of Social Studies and Literacy," in Margit E. McGuire and Bronwyn Cole (eds.), *Making a Difference: Revitalizing Elementary Social Studies* (Silver Spring, MD: National Council for the Social Studies Bulletin 109): 51.

5. Paula Overland Brandt and Rahima Wade, "Made for Each Other: Social Studies and Children's Literature," *Social Studies and the Young Learner* 8, No. 2 (November-December 1995): 18-20.

6. Barbara Brenner, *If You Were There in 1492: Everyday Life in the Time of Columbus* (New York: Simon and Schuster, Aladdin,1998).

7. The early grades specified in the standards include grades pre-K-4, while grade 5 is included in the middle level.

3 Connecting National Curriculum Standards, Reading Skills, and Social Studies Content

Peggy Altoff and Charlee Archuleta

The previous chapter suggested some useful criteria for selecting literature for teaching social studies. This chapter will identify key skills that teachers should seek to develop in elementary students in order to enhance their reading and conceptual abilities in social studies and provide them with the opportunity for excellence.

The *National Curriculum Standards for Social Studies* include an appendix on "Essential Social Studies Skills and Strategies," which lists eighteen literacy skills.[1] These skills are presented on p. 10 of this book. The standards point out that "teachers emphasize certain aspects of literacy over others, depending on the nature of the content and skills they want students to learn."[2]

The standards also recommend some broad-based literacy strategies that teachers can employ to improve their students' comprehension of written sources.[3] The standards volume points out that "it is best to teach and practice these while students engage in learning challenging content," and recommends dividing them into the following three categories before, during and after reading a text:[4]

Before

▶ Reviewing vocabulary that will be encountered in the reading

▶ Connecting to students' prior knowledge

▶ Making predictions about what the text might say

▶ Identifying text features including headings, charts/graphs/tables, illustrations, and maps

▶ Setting targets or objectives

During

▶ Drawing a non-linguistic representation, or image

▶ Asking questions about key ideas

▶ Identifying unfamiliar ideas, concepts, or words to work with later

▶ Using questions, cues, and advance organizers

After

▶ Summarizing and note-taking

▶ Comparing notes with those of other students

▶ Providing substantive homework and practice

▶ Reinforcing effort and providing recognition

This chapter will focus on five of the literacy skills outlined in the *National Curriculum Standards for Social Studies* which are emphasized in core reading programs and assessments for elementary students, as well as in state social studies standards and texts. They are an essential component of social studies education at the elementary level. A natural connection exists between these literacy skills, social studies content, and the common core reading standards, and teachers can take advantage of this by using "before, during and after" strategies to enhance student comprehension of a variety of texts and sources. The five skills are:

- Arrange events in chronological sequence
- Analyze cause and effect relationships
- Determine and analyze similarities and differences
- Describe people, places, and events and the connections between and among them
- Define and apply discipline-based conceptual vocabulary

1. Chronology and Sequence

Chronology is always sequence, but sequence is not always chronology. Chronology, simply defined, is arranging events in the order in which they happened: for example, a listing of colonies in order of the dates they were founded, or the order of events leading to the American Revolution. Sequence, as found in many reading programs, can include chronology, but often refers to a logical series of steps to complete a task, such as making a peanut butter and jelly sandwich, stirring up a pitcher of lemonade, or wrapping a package. The skill of arranging events chronologically is emphasized in social studies, specifically in Theme 2, **TIME, CONTINUITY AND CHANGE**, as students learn to locate themselves in time and study the past. The Common Core Reading Standards for Literature and the Common Core Reading Standards for Informational Text also emphasize the skills of being able to recall and connect events, and a Common Core Reading

Standard for Literature (Grade 3) explicitly cites the need for students to "describe characters in a story (e.g., their traits, motivations, or feelings), and explain how their actions contribute to a sequence of events."[5] A later chapter of this book, which focuses on the story *The Little House*, provides an application of this skill for the second grade classroom. (See Chapter 8)

Table 1 outlines one approach to teaching chronology.

Before Students Read

Introducing chronology to younger students involves having them think about daily happenings in their own lives, and should include very concrete experiences:

- Use events such as getting up in the morning, having lunch, playing, eating dinner, and going to bed. Assign each of these to students, and finally have them arrange themselves in the order that the events happened. Ask questions: which came first? Which was second? Which was last? What other events in your daily lives could you add to this timeline?
- Consider using the events of everyday classroom life. School begins at ___ a.m., and so on, through morning warm-up, reading instruction, recess, lunch, art class, math class, closing activities and departure for the day at ___ p.m. Use word cards

Table 1: Approach to Teaching Chronology		
SKILL	**CLUE WORDS**	**QUESTIONS TO ASK WHEN PREPARING TO TEACH**
Chronology - What is chronology? - How will students demonstrate that they understand the skill?	- First, second, third - Before, after - Next, then - While - As soon as - Finally - In 1776 - By noon - Until 10 p.m.	- What are the events students will study? - What is the correct order of these events? - Why is it important that they be placed in the correct order? - What are the relationships among these events?

with the name of the activity on the front and a picture of a clock on the back. Have students arrange themselves in order of the word activities, then have them turn the cards over to check if their times are in the correct order as well.

▶ Learn the days of the week and the months of the year. Place well known events in chronological order—Thanksgiving, Christmas, Easter, children's birthdays.

Introducing this skill and reinforcing it among older elementary school children should include a review of earlier learning, and the following instructions:

▶ Define chronology and apply the idea to their own lives by listing events in the correct order from birth through current grade;

▶ Emphasize the past, present, and future, by defining each term and applying to events in their own lives;

▶ Arrange events in their towns or communities in the order that they happened;

▶ Complete timelines of significant events in the history of the state or nation.

During Reading

When using one or more of the books in the following chapters, list important events that happened. For younger students, use three or four events and scramble them to see if the students can place them in order. Create a simple timeline, using large index cards, string, and paper clips or clothespins so they can see the timeline spatially. Be sure to discuss why the events are important, and how they are connected.

Upper elementary students can be given a scrambled list of events from a chapter of literature or informational text, which they read to determine the chronology. Work with them to draw a simple timeline, which could also be illustrated with drawings of events. Be sure to discuss why the events are important and how they are connected to reinforce their understanding of the timeline.

After Reading

At the level at which students begin formal assessments that involve multiple choice questions, use the types of questions typically found on standardized tests. It is important to help learners prepare for the types of questions they will encounter. For example, provide a short reading passage, and a question: Which event happened first or which event happened last? Provide the four typical response options, i.e. A,B,C,D.

Teachers need to determine whether students actually grasp the skill by having them demonstrate their understanding in a novel situation. For younger students, a series of school events in a given week might be provided, and students asked to place them in the correct order. For older students, a new reading passage on the topic under study can be used, along with directions to select a number of events and place them correctly on a timeline.

2. Cause and Effect

At a basic level, this skill involves focusing on an event, determining why that event occurred, and identifying the result(s). In the social studies standards, the skill is often tied to Theme 2, **TIME, CONTINUITY, AND CHANGE**, as students learn to locate themselves in time and study the past. Connections with other themes can, however, easily be made. One example addresses Theme 3, **PEOPLE, PLACES, AND ENVIRONMENTS**. When students study Native American migration from Asia to North America, they should understand both the causes and effects of this migration.

The Common Core English Language Arts Standards, which repeatedly emphasize the need for students to develop skills in describing connections between individuals, events, ideas, and places, put a high value on skills that lead to an understanding of cause and effect. The Reading Standards for Informational Text specifically cite the need for fourth and fifth graders to understand "cause/effect."[6] The activities presented in chapter 8 for reading the book, *The Little House,* offer an application of this skill.

Table 2: Teaching About Cause and Effect

SKILL	CLUE WORDS	QUESTIONS TO ASK WHEN PREPARING TO TEACH
Cause and Effect ▸ What is a cause? What is an effect? ▸ How will students demonstrate that they understand the skill?	▸ Because ▸ Since ▸ So ▸ If ▸ Therefore ▸ As a result ▸ Consequently ▸ Nevertheless	▸ What happened? ▸ Why did it happen? ▸ What are the results?

Table 2 indicates one approach to teaching about cause and effect.

Before Students Read

Introducing the skill should involve a simple event in your life or the life of a student. One example might include you telling students that you were late to school this morning. Ask them why you might have been late and expect responses such as your alarm did not ring, there was an emergency at home, you could not find your keys, or there was an accident. Next, ask what this might mean for the rest of your day, with responses including that your work may not get done or their work might not get graded. Introduce the terms *event* (what happens), *cause* (why an event happens), and *effect* (the result[s]), and apply them to this situation. Next, select an event common to students' lives, e.g., a low grade on an assignment (the *event*), failing to study (*cause*), having to work harder, or having to redo the assignment (*result*). Finally, apply the terms to a topic or text under current study. You might also select a chronology or time line that students completed, and apply the skill by making connections among the events illustrated.

Another example, particularly appropriate for younger students, involves introducing the same vocabulary of *event, cause,* and *effect*, and placing the terms on word cards. Set up a flannel board or magnetic board so that students may see the words and pictures in order as they are added to the board. Use pictures of a familiar event to show students how events have a cause and effect, such as an apple falling from a tree (event) because of a high wind (cause), then hitting the ground so hard that it creates a brown spot on the apple (effect). Students must match the correct terms with each part of the example.

During Reading

When using one or more of the books in the following chapters, or any other text, focus on a single event that you select. With students, determine a cause and an effect of that event. Next, select an event that has more than one cause and more than one effect and have students identify these. Encourage students to be realistic, but also creative in their ideas of possible causes and effects, to move them beyond a basic understanding. The ability to complete this task will depend upon the skill levels of learners. If possible, select two related events, and work with students to determine that one is the cause or result of the other. There are a variety of graphic organizers that can be used to assist students with this task:

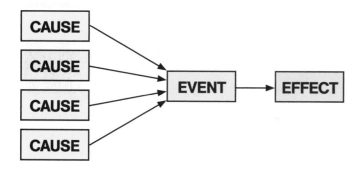

The number of causes that are used on the graphic organizer will vary depending upon the text used. The same is true for the graphic below.

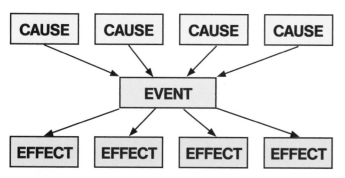

For students at the intermediate level, this organizer may prove useful. Again, it can be altered by adding or removing boxes, depending on the text being used.

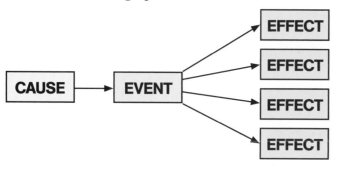

For students at the intermediate level, a graphic organizer that shows how an effect can be a cause of another event might also help increase understanding.

Once students have identified causes and effects of an event, asking higher level questions helps to increase understanding. Which cause was most important and why? Which was the least important? Which effect was most important? Least important? Which effect became the cause of another event? If you reread the text, what other cause might you add? What about the event? How could you use a time line to illustrate the causes and effects of this event?

After Reading
Use the types of questions typically found on standardized tests. For example, provide a short reading passage, and a question: Which of the following was a cause of the event or which of the following was an effect? Provide the four typical response options (i.e., A,B,C,D), for each question.

To determine if students actually grasp the skill, have them demonstrate their understanding in a unique situation. For younger students, a school event might be provided, such as a team winning a sports contest, with students asked to identify a cause and effect. For older students, a new reading passage on the topic under study can be used, along with directions to select an event, and identify both the cause(s) and effect(s).

3. Similarities and Differences
Research has shown that student proficiency in identifying similarities and differences increases student understanding and achievement.[7] This skill is associated with the processes of comparing and contrasting, creating metaphors, completing analogies, and classifying information. The focus here will be on comparing and contrasting.[8] This skill can be tied to all NCSS Standard themes, but notably those of ❶ CULTURE; ❷ TIME, CONTINUITY, AND CHANGE; ❸ PEOPLE, PLACES, AND ENVIRONMENTS; ❻ POWER, AUTHORITY, AND GOVERNANCE; and ❼ PRODUCTION, DISTRIBUTION, AND CONSUMPTION. In the Common Core English Language Arts Standards, this skill can be found in the Reading Standards for Literature, which cite the ability to "compare and contrast" at all K-5 grade levels, as well as in relevant

Table 3: Teaching About Comparison and Contrast

SKILL	CLUE WORDS	QUESTIONS TO ASK WHEN PREPARING TO TEACH
Comparing and Contrasting ▶ What do students compare and contrast? ▶ How will students demonstrate that they understand the skill?	▶ Alike ▶ Different, unlike ▶ Similar ▶ Relatively ▶ While ▶ Either…or ▶ But ▶ On the other hand	▶ What is being compared and contrasted (people, places, events, ideas, etc.)? ▶ What are the characteristics used to compare and contrast? ▶ How are they alike or similar? ▶ How are they different?

sections of the Reading Standards for Informational Text.[9] The activities for the books *You and Me Together* and *Nina Bonita* in Chapters 5 and 7 of this book offer examples of the application of this skill.

Table 3 indicates one approach to teaching about comparison and contrast.

Before Students Read

Introducing the skill involves modeling the process with content familiar to students. First, choose the content, such as pictures of a cat and a dog. Then, establish the traits or attributes on which to base the comparison, such as food, sounds, size, activities, etc. Next, record information in each category for each animal. Using a simple graphic organizer can assist students with this task:

Graphic Organizer

CHARACTERISTIC	CAT	DOG
food		
sounds		
size		
activities		

Completion of an organizer should be followed by discussing how the animals are alike and different. Depending on the age/ability level of the group, a third column could be added for rabbit, guinea pig, snake or a widely owned pet. In order to put the activity in familiar context and require greater attention to detail, introduction to the skill can also be accomplished by having two female or male students from the class stand side by side, then creating the same chart and showing what students see as similarities and differences between each child.

Repeat the entire process with a topic currently under study, allowing students to select the characteristics for comparison and to work independently to record information in their charts. If students fail to select all characteristics that you had in mind, ask them to add another row to the bottom of the chart. Then review the text in use to add another characteristic, or supply them with one they may have missed. Students can pair/share information before a class discussion summarizing likenesses and differences. Again, depending on the age and ability level of students, they could write a summary of one or more sentences to compare and contrast the people, places, events, or ideas in their charts.

During Reading

When using one or more of the books in the following chapters, or other text, identify the content—people, places, events, ideas, etc.—that you want students to compare and contrast. You can provide a graphic organizer or ask students to create one. The Venn Diagram is a popular tool for applying this skill, as is a T-chart, or a graphic organizer like that shown on page 24. Again, depending on the age/ability level of the group, a third circle or column could be added to include another item for comparison/contrast to the first two.

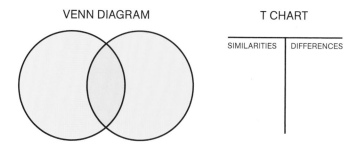

VENN DIAGRAM   T CHART

SIMILARITIES | DIFFERENCES

After Reading

Always follow the completion of a graphic organizer with a summary of the likeness and differences recorded. Also ask students how the items compared/contrasted are most alike and most different. To assess, use the types of questions typically found on standardized tests. For example, provide a short reading passage about two people, places, events, or ideas, and a question: *How are _____ and _____ alike?* Or, *How are _____ and _____ different?* Provide the four typical response options (i.e. A, B, C, D), for each question.

To determine if students actually grasp the skill, have them demonstrate their understanding in a unique situation. Students can be given a different text, or part of a text that is purposefully selected to meet the purpose of comparing and contrasting. Specific directions should be provided:

▸ Compare and contrast these two _____ by choosing and completing a graphic organizer, then summarizing your work by writing two or more sentences about how ___ and ___ are alike and different.

Depending on the skill level of the learners, the organizer can be provided and the number of summary sentences changed.

4. Descriptions of People, Places, and Environments

A description or account of an event involves reporting or sketching people, places, events, or ideas with accurate and appropriate detail. It also includes explaining the connections between and among the people, places, events, or ideas under study. This skill is invariably linked with the reading skill of identifying the main idea. In any reading, and at every grade level, students should be asked, "What is this reading about?" Then, students should be asked to elaborate by adding details to that main idea. The elaboration should include terms from what has been read. Often teachers need to ask follow-up questions in order to get students to add details. For example, a text on Benedict Arnold might focus on the actions that led him to betray his country during the American Revolution. After eliciting this information, additional questions include: *Why? What actions did he take? Where did this happen? How did his actions impact those of others?* This skill can be tied to all NCSS Standards themes, but notably to ❶ CULTURE; ❷ TIME, CONTINUITY AND CHANGE; ❸ PEOPLE, PLACES, AND ENVIRONMENTS; and ❻ POWER, AUTHORITY AND GOVERNANCE. In the common core standards, this skill is emphasized in both Reading Standards for Literature and Reading Standards for Informational Text.[10] The activities for *Sarah, Plain and Tall* in Chapter 11 offer an application of this skill.

Table 4 (p. 26) indicates one approach to teaching about description.

Before Students Read

Introducing any skill involves modeling a process using familiar content. For primary grades, start with a picture, such as a farm scene. Ask students what the picture shows, i.e. what is this about? Identify the correct response as the *main idea*, e.g., life on a farm. Then ask what they see in the picture—fields of corn, cows, a tractor, etc. Identify these as *details*.

For intermediate level students, select a short paragraph. Read it to students, then have them reread it independently. Ask the most important question: *What*

Table 4: Teaching About Description

SKILL	CLUE WORDS	QUESTIONS TO ASK WHEN PREPARING TO TEACH
Description ▶ How do students describe people, events, places, ideas? ▶ How will students demonstrate that they understand the skill?	▶ For instance ▶ For example ▶ Such as ▶ To illustrate ▶ Most important ▶ In addition ▶ Another ▶ Also ▶ In fact	▶ What is being described? What is the reading about? ▶ What are the details about the people, events, places, ideas in the passage? ▶ What words or terms can be used to expand or elaborate on this description?

is this about? Identify the correct response as the *main idea* of the passage, and record this term along with the appropriate response. Next, begin to elicit details about this main idea by asking: *What else can you tell me about___?* Depending upon the topic, the standard six questions can be addressed: *Who? What? When? Where? Why? How?* Encourage students to use any special terms or words that are part of the passage as they respond to questions. Identify the responses as *details* that lead to better understanding of the main idea. Depending on the age and level of students, you might also wish to use a picture that is rich in action and details, and repeat the process.

Replicate the entire process with a paragraph or more from a topic currently under study, with students asking the question that will lead to understanding the main idea: *What is this reading about?* Expand student thinking by asking the questions that elicit details, with emphasis on words or terms that are key to understanding. A simple graphic organizer can be used to record information:

> **Title of Reading**
> ▶ Main Idea: What is this about?
> ▶ Details: (Who? What? When? Where? Why? How?)
>   ...
>   ...
>   ...

As students become familiar with the skill, add paragraphs and/or expand the reading selections so that they can identify main ideas and details from a section or chapter. At this point, additional questions should be introduced and discussed: *How are the main ideas of the sections/chapters connected? How are the people, places, events, and ideas in the sections/chapters connected?*

During Reading

When using one or more of the books in the following chapters, or other text, identify the content—people, places, events, ideas, etc.—in paragraphs, pictures, sections or chapters that you want to use to have students apply the skill. Provide a simple graphic organizer for a short passage or picture. If working with a section or chapter, consider one that is more complex (see below). Depending on the age and level of the student, the sample offered below can be adapted so that there are two, three, or four parts to complete.

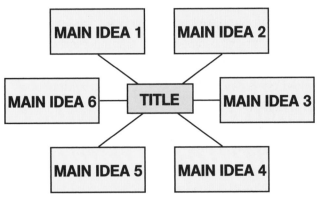

When students have finalized the information recorded in any graphic organizer, they can work in pairs or triads to discuss their work. It is also important to discuss their findings as a class and to establish connections among the various main ideas. The details can be used to achieve these goals.

After Reading

To assess, use the types of questions typically found on standardized tests. Provide students with a short reading passage (which can be made longer for students who are older or at an appropriate ability level) about a person, place, event, or idea and a question: What is the main idea of the paragraph/passage? Provide the four typical response options (i.e. A, B, C, D), for each question.

To determine if students have fully grasped the skill, have them demonstrate their understanding in a unique situation. Provide a picture or a reading passage about a person, place, event, or idea. Specific directions should be provided: Describe what is happening in this picture or passage by explaining the main idea and providing two or more details that support the main idea.

5. Define and Apply Conceptual Vocabulary

This topic is related to all others discussed in this chapter. The common core standards emphasize the importance of vocabulary development. Conceptual vocabulary includes concepts, ideas, and terms that are essential to understanding social studies content. It requires a depth of knowledge and understanding that goes beyond mere recognition, definition, and use in a sentence. The development of conceptual vocabulary requires explicit and intentional instruction. Words such as causality, region, democracy, and scarcity are essential to understanding the respective NCSS Standards themes of ❶ TIME, CONTINUITY, AND CHANGE; ❸ PEOPLE, PLACES, AND ENVIRONMENTS; ❻ POWER, AUTHORITY, AND GOVERNANCE; and ❼ PRODUCTION, DISTRIBUTION, AND CONSUMPTION. Although some sources that focus on vocabulary instruction include lists of people and places—which are very important to the study of social studies—these are not part of students' conceptual vocabulary and should be addressed separately. Vocabulary strategies can and should be applied as you work with each of the books selected for the following chapters.

Volumes have been written on strategies to use with students and there are an abundance of resources, both print and electronic, to assist teachers with student mastery of vocabulary. One that teachers may find particularly useful is www.justreadnow. com/strategies/vocabulary.htm. Clear explanations are provided for fourteen separate strategies, along with a step-by-step process for teaching each of them and a list of resources to consult for learning more. It is important to use a variety of strategies and activities to engage students in active learning and maintain interest.

Here are some suggestions to consider when helping students acquire conceptual vocabulary:

▶ Focus on vocabulary that is essential to mastering content and concepts. For example, if the reading is about colonization of the Americas, the ideas expressed in *colony, colonist, colonization* are key. The phrases *joint stock company* or *proprietary colony* may be important in the short term, for understanding the content in a section or chapter, but not for long term memory and application. These words are usually highlighted for students and definitions provided to aid immediate understanding

▶ Avoid words that students have no opportunity to use or that cannot be explained in easy-to-use language. Choose vocabulary that continues to be applicable in other times and places, including the present. Thus, using the example above, students will learn about the *colonization* of Africa, South America and/or Asia later in their studies.

▶ Limit the amount of conceptual vocabulary selected for teaching and learning. Research has shown that, on average, children can acquire and retain 2-3 new words a day when taught in context and followed with explanations.[11] This suggests that the choice of conceptual vocabulary as part of classroom instruction should be careful and selective. Further incidental learning of vocabulary can also occur at home, among peers, or through community experience.

- Have students use conceptual vocabulary as often as possible—for example, in discussions, in writing, or on word walls. Oral language is an essential element of the future use of vocabulary. If students are able to use the selected vocabulary in dialogue and/or discussion, they are more apt to use it in writing, in future lessons and in life.

- Have students create images to illustrate the meanings of words. Research supports the notion that students acquire vocabulary that they associate with mental images. Note that these should be appropriate and accurate, but owned by students. They may not be able to associate meaning with images created by teachers.

- While it may seem obvious, the conceptual vocabulary selected for mastery should consist of words and terms that students will encounter when learning new content. The days when teachers provided students a random list to pronounce, write five times, define, use in a sentence, and take a test in order to determine mastery should be long gone. The list should be short, meaningful, and applicable on a daily, weekly, monthly, and yearly basis.

- Beyond the scope of conceptual vocabulary, students should be allowed to have fun with words, and to select one word or term, or more, each week that appeals to them because it sounds funny, is spelled funny, or has a unique meaning. A special word wall in the classroom should be available for students to record these, and an opportunity provided to share with others. When possible, allow students to act out what the words are or mean; movement can further enrich their understanding. Teachers can use this opportunity to show their own love of words by sharing their favorites.

These suggestions are designed to engage the reader in thinking about current practice. The list is not definitive, and other sources should be consulted as each teacher constructs a list of practical pointers that are applicable in a specific classroom for a specific group of learners at a specific grade level. It is always important to remember that knowledge of conceptual vocabulary increases reading comprehension, and reading increases vocabulary.

A distinct pattern has been employed in addressing the skills selected for inclusion in this chapter. It is one that is suitable for teaching students any skill:

- Introduce the skill using familiar content so that it will be easy for students to acquire

- Guide students in their initial and subsequent applications to topics currently being studied

- Apply the skill in new situations after students have acquired some confidence in using the skill

- Use before-during-after strategies, including graphic organizers, to assist students in reaching mastery

- Assess students in at least two ways: first, assess the skill as it would be assessed on a standardized test, so that students become familiar with the usual format of these tests; second, assess the skill in a way that demonstrates mastery of the skill.

Classroom instruction that promotes the skills identified in this chapter, when combined with the right selection of literature, will give elementary students the opportunity to excel in social studies. 📓

NOTES
1. National Council for the Social Studies (NCSS), *National Curriculum Standards for Social Studies: A Framework for Teaching, Learning, and Assessment* (Silver Spring, MD: NCSS, 2010), 163.

2. *Ibid.*

3. *Ibid.*, 165.

4. *Ibid.*

5. National Governors Association Center for Best Practices and Council of Chief State School Officers, *Common Core State Standards for English Language Arts and Literacy in History/Social Studies, Science, and Technical Subjects* (Washington, D.C.: National Governors Association Center for Best Practices and Council of Chief State School Officers, 2010), 12.

6. There is an emphasis on connections in the Key Ideas and Details section (Item 3) of both the Common Core Standards for Reading Literature and the Common Core Standards for Reading Informational Text. The latter set of standards explicitly refers to cause/effect in Item 5 (Craft and Structure) for Grades 4 and 5. See *Common Core State Standards for English Language Arts and Literacy in History/Social Studies, Science, and Technical Subjects*, 11-14.

7. Ceri B. Dean et al., *Classroom Instruction That Works* (Alexandria, VA: ASCD and McREL, 2012), 119.

8. Some states and districts define *comparison* as the ability to recognize likenesses and differences, while others define *comparison* as the ability to recognize likenesses and *contrast* as the ability to recognize differences. The latter will be used in this publication as students compare and contrast people, places, events, ideas, etc.

9. *Common Core State Standards for English Language Arts and Literacy in History/Social Studies, Science, and Technical Subjects*, 11-14. Item 9 of the Reading Standards for Literature, "Integration of Knowledge and Ideas," outlines "compare and contrast" objectives for all K-5 Grades.

10. *Ibid.*, 11-14. See the Key Ideas and Details for each set of standards, especially Item 3.

11. See, for example, the article by Andrew Biemiller, "Teaching Vocabulary—Early, Direct, and Sequential," originally published in *Perspectives* 26, no. 4 (Fall 2000) and reprinted in *American Educator* (Spring 2001). The article is accessible in the *American Educator* archives at http://www.aft.org/newspubs/periodicals/ae/spring2001/biemiller.cfm.

Part 2

Outstanding Children's Literature For Teaching Social Studies

4 How To Use Part 2 of This Book

In the chapters that follow in Part 2 of this volume, teachers will find a rich selection of outstanding children's books that are useful both for meeting the national social studies standards and for promoting specific objectives of the Common Core Standards for English Language Arts in grades K through 5. The chapters offer integrated units based on excellent and engaging books, and describe in detail how teachers can maximize the potential of these books for teaching social studies as well as English Language Arts. One chapter deals with each elementary grade level from Kindergarten to Grade 5. Each chapter opens by identifying the theme or themes of the social studies standards that can be taught using the main featured book.

Each of the seven chapters that deal with a specific grade level analyzes an outstanding book in depth and offers teachers two activities based on the book that meet designated social studies standards, as well as a set of strategies for using the book to teach to the Common Core Reading Standards for Literature for that grade level. To ensure that all ten social studies themes are covered at each grade level, each chapter also annotates books dealing with the nine social studies themes that are not the primary focus of the main activity based on the featured book.

Each chapter opens by identifying the theme or themes of the social studies standards that can be taught using the main featured book. The following example is from Chapter 10.

The first page of each chapter also identifies the Common Core Standards that can be met by the set of English Language Arts activities presented in the chapter. The following example is from Chapter 6 on Kindergarten.

Social Studies Standards Themes
❶ CULTURE
❸ PEOPLE, PLACES, AND ENVIRONMENTS

Other Related Themes
❷ TIME, CONTINUITY, AND CHANGE
❽ SCIENCE, TECHNOLOGY, AND SOCIETY

Common Core Standards

READING: LITERATURE—KINDERGARTEN
Key Ideas and Details
1. With prompting and support, ask and answer questions about key details in a text.

Craft and Structure
4. Ask and answer questions about unknown words in a text.

READING: FOUNDATIONAL SKILLS—KINDERGARTEN
Phonological Awareness
2. Demonstrate understanding of spoken words, syllables, and sounds (phonemes)
(a) Recognize and produce rhyming words.

LANGUAGE—KINDERGARTEN
Conventions of Standard English
1. Demonstrate command of the conventions of standard English grammar and usage when writing or speaking....

At the start of each social studies activity, teachers will find a list of the learning expectations of the social studies standards that the activity helps to meet. The following example is from Chapter 8 for Grade 2.

NCSS Curriculum Standard
❷ TIME, CONTINUITY, AND CHANGE

QUESTION FOR EXPLORATION EARLY GRADES
▶ How was life in the past similar to and different from life today?

PROCESSES EARLY GRADES
Learners will be able to...
▶ Identify examples of both continuity and change, as demonstrated in stories, photographs, and documents

PRODUCTS EARLY GRADES
Learners demonstrate understanding by...
▶ Constructing timelines that indicate an understanding of a sequence of events.

Likewise at the start of the English Language Arts activities, teachers will find a list of the Common Core Reading Standards for Literature that the activities help to meet. This example is also from Chapter 8.

Some chapters also recommend strategies that teachers can use with the book to help to meet other selected Common Core standards (e.g., for Reading: Foundational Skills, Language, and Writing). This example is from Chapter 11 for Grade 5.

Common Core Standards

READING: LITERATURE—GRADE 2
Key Ideas and Details
1. Ask and answer questions such as *who, what, where, when, why,* and *how* to demonstrate understanding of key details in a text.
3. Describe how characters in a story respond to major events and challenges.

Craft and Structure
5. Describe the overall structure of a story, including describing how the beginning introduces the story and the ending concludes

LANGUAGE—GRADE 5
Vocabulary Acquisition and Use
4. Determine or clarify the meaning of unknown and multiple-meaning words and phrases based on *grade 5 reading and content*, choosing flexibly from a range of strategies.

WRITING—GRADE 5
Text Types and Purposes
2. Write informative/explanatory texts to examine a topic and convey ideas and information clearly.

Production and Distribution of Writing
4. Produce clear and coherent writing in which the development and organization are appropriate to task, purpose, and audience.

It is left to the discretion of the teacher to determine the order in which the activities should be taught, or how to blend them together. By presenting the social studies activities first, we do not imply that they should precede the English Language Arts activities, but we do wish to emphasize that the books are valuable for the social studies curriculum, and the teacher should ensure that the social studies activities do not "fall out" in favor of the English Language Arts activities.

After the main activities of each chapter, an annotated list of books recommends at least one book for each of the ten themes of the social studies that is not the main theme of the first social studies activity presented in the chapter.

The annotations include a question for exploration drawn directly from the social studies standards that can be used to organize class activities related to the book, such as this example from Chapter 9 for Grade 3.

❽ SCIENCE, TECHNOLOGY, AND SOCIETY

Gene Baretta, *Neo Leo: The Ageless Ideas of Leonardo da Vinci* (New York: Henry Holt and Company, 2009)

Leonardo's notebooks show that he thought of ideas for helicopters, tanks, hang gliders, contact lenses, robots and more — centuries before they were actually built.

QUESTION FOR EXPLORATION: What are some examples of science and technology that have impacted individuals and society?

At the end of each chapter, there are references to another set of English Language Arts standards that the books recommended in the chapter can help to meet: *Standards for the English Language Arts*, published in 1996 by the International Reading Association (IRA) and National Council of Teachers of English (NCTE). The following example is from the end of Chapter 8.

The books cited in this chapter are recommended for their value in implementing the National Curriculum Standards for Social Studies and the Common Core State Standards for English Language Arts in Grade 2. They can also be used to help to meet the following standards from the national Standards for the English Language Arts published in 1996 by the International Reading Association and National Council of Teachers of English.

2 Students read a wide range of literature from many periods in many genres to build an understanding of many dimensions (e.g., philosophical, ethical, aesthetic) of human experience.

3 Students apply a wide range of strategies to comprehend, interpret, evaluate, and appreciate texts. They draw on their prior experience, their interactions with other readers and writers, their knowledge of word meaning and of other texts, their word identification strategies, and their understanding of textual features (e.g., sound-letter correspondence, sentence structure, context, graphics)

A bibliography at the end of the book (pp. 109–115) offers recommendations of scores of other books that can be used to teach the ten themes of social studies. The following recommendations for Grade 1 are an example.

First Grade

Barnwell, Ysaye M. *We Are One.* Illus. by Brian Pinkney. Orlando: Harcourt, 2008. 32 pp.
❾ GLOBAL CONNECTIONS

Bottner, Barbara. *Miss Brooks Loves Books! (and I Don't).* Illus. by Michael Emberley. New York: Knopf, 2010. 32 pp.
❹ INDIVIDUAL DEVELOPMENT AND IDENTITY

Caseley, Judith. *On the Town: A Community Adventure.* New York: HarperCollins, Greenwillow, 2002. Unp.
❻ POWER, AUTHORITY, AND GOVERNANCE

Cooper, Elisha. *Farm.* New York: Orchard Books, 2010. 32 pp.
❸ PEOPLE, PLACES, AND ENVIRONMENTS

Doner, Kim. *On a Road in Africa.* Berkeley, CA: Tricycle Press, 2008. 48 pp.
❸ PEOPLE, PLACES, AND ENVIRONMENTS

Gerdner, Linda and Sarah Langford. *Grandfather's Story Cloth.* Illus. by Stuart Loughridge. Walnut Creek, CA: Shen's Books, 2008. 32 pp.
❷ TIME, CONTINUITY, AND CHANGE

Hoberman, Mary Ann. *You Read to Me, I'll Read to You: Very Short Fairy Tales to Read Together (in which wolves are tamed, trolls are transformed, and peas are triumphant.)* Illus. by Michael Emberley. New York: Little, Brown/Megan Tingley, 2004. 32 pp.
❹ INDIVIDUAL DEVELOPMENT AND IDENTITY

Jenkins, Steve. *Never Smile at a Monkey: and 17 Other Important Things to Remember.* Boston: Houghton Mifflin Books for Children, 2009. Unp.
❸ PEOPLE, PLACES, AND ENVIRONMENTS

Jules, Jacqueline. *Duck for Turkey Day.* Illus. by Kathryn Mitter. Morton Grove, IL: Albert Whitman & Co., 2009. Unp.
❶ CULTURE

Krull, Kathleen. *Supermarket.* Illus. by Melanie Hope Greenberg. New York: Holiday House, 2001. Unp.
❼ PRODUCTION, CONSUMPTION, AND DISTRIBUTION

O'Neill, Alexis. *The Recess Queen.* Illus. by Laura Huliska-Beith. New York: Scholastic, 2002. Unp.
❻ POWER, AUTHORITY, AND GOVERNANCE

Peete, Holly Robinson and Ryan Elizabeth Peete with Denene Millner. *My Brother Charlie.* Pictures by Shane W. Evans. New York: Scholastic Press, 2010. 36 pp.
❹ INDIVIDUAL DEVELOPMENT AND IDENTITY

Reynolds, Aaron. *Metal Man.* Illus. by Paul Hoppe. Watertown, MA: Charlesbridge, 2008. 32 pp.
❶ CULTURE

Scieszka, Jon. *Truckery Rhymes.* Illus. by David Shannon, Loren Long, David Gordon and others. New York: Simon & Schuster, 2009. 57 pp.
❽ SCIENCE, TECHNOLOGY, AND SOCIETY

Sheth, Kashmira. *Monsoon Afternoon.* Illus. by Yoshiko Jaeggi. Atlanta, GA: Peachtree Publishers, 2008. 32 pp.
❸ PEOPLE, PLACES, AND ENVIRONMENTS

Sidman, Joyce. *Red Sings from Treetops: a Year in Colors.* Illus. by Pamela Zagarenski. Boston: Houghton Mifflin Books for Children, 2009. Unp.
❸ PEOPLE, PLACES, AND ENVIRONMENTS

Simon, Norma. *All Kinds of Children.* Illus. by Diane Paterson. Morton Grove, IL: Albert Whitman & Co, 1999. 32 pp.
❾ GLOBAL CONNECTIONS

Solheim, James. *Born Yesterday: The Diary of a Young Journalist.* Illus. by Simon James. New York: Penguin, Philomel, 2010. unp.
❹ INDIVIDUAL DEVELOPMENT AND IDENTITY

Wolff, Ashley. *I Call My Grandma Nana.* Berkeley, CA: Tricycle Press, 2009. 30 pp.
❶ CULTURE

Wolff, Ashley. *I Call My Grandpa Papa.* Berkeley, CA: Tricycle Press, 2009. 30 pp.
❶ CULTURE

You and Me Together: Moms, Dads, and Kids Around the World

Written by Barbara Kerley

Washington, DC: National Geographic Children's Books, 2005

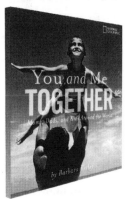

Readers of all ages are drawn immediately to this nonfiction book written for young learners, which offers exquisite photographs of children engaging in a wide variety of special activities with one of their parents. The book was selected as an NCSS Notable Social Studies Trade Book for Young People in 2006.

Photographed in 24 different locations around the world, each picture conveys the joy of the moment as a child and parent partake in daily events such as sharing a story or a joke, playing a musical instrument or a game, or taking a walk or a nap. Pictures show people from diverse cultures in colorful clothing participating in a typical activity in their home environments. The child-with-parent exchanges are featured in places such as Australia, Brazil, China, Iceland, India, Italy, Japan, Saudi Arabia, Uganda, and the United States.

Written for preschool through second grade readers, the text uses a repeated lyrical pattern beginning with present participles, action words that end with *–ing*. The action words are followed by a variety of activities, extending the action word with an object, yet the objects are unrelated to one another. For example, in one set of photographs, the children and parents are shown holding a hand, a pet, or a rake. In this case, the action word is "hold." From these words and photographs, young readers will be eager to add activities that finish the action word with objects resonating with their lives and experiences. Thoughtfully, the book focuses on one child and one parent on each page, reflective of today's world where many young children spend their time with only one adult.

You and Me Together: Moms, Dads, and Kids Around the World includes two special features. At the end of the book, the author has included a map of the world. Each location shown in a photograph in the book is identified on the map. These pages also include smaller versions of the photographs from the text. Each of the smaller photographs is accompanied by a few sentences describing the events portrayed in the

---

Social Studies Standards Themes

❹ **INDIVIDUAL DEVELOPMENT AND IDENTITY**

❺ **INDIVIDUALS, GROUPS, AND INSTITUTIONS**

❾ **GLOBAL CONNECTIONS**

Common Core Standards

READING: LITERATURE—KINDERGARTEN

(There are no reading standards for Pre-K)

Key Ideas and Details

1. With prompting and support, ask and answer questions about key details in a text.

Craft and Structure

4. Ask and answer questions about unknown words in a text.

Range of Reading and Level of Text Complexity

10. Actively engage in group reading activities with purpose and understanding.

photograph, conveyed with specialized vocabulary and information about the people, activities, and objects.

The second feature at the end of the book is a note authored by Marian Wright Edelman, president of the Children's Defense Fund. In her note, Ms. Edelman emphasizes the need for a "world of parents who love all children" by "offering a helping hand to a community and nation of children." She encourages the reader to "open your eyes and hearts to energize and organize." The note also includes statistics about the world's population, providing a context for children and their challenges around the world.

Reading the book aloud to young children will enable them to hear about common child and parent activities shared around the world by young children just like them, and to see beautiful scenes of places most young learners have never seen or imagined. The book increases awareness of similarities and differences locally and globally. It shows the objects featured with the action words, and relates cultural competence in ways that are honest, authentic, natural, and holistic. Reading the book aloud will spark conversations and initiate learning experiences that explore child and parent interactions familiar to the listeners. Young children can share these with one another to advance conversations and understandings.

Teachers can use *You and Me Together: Moms, Dads, and Kids Around the World* to highlight two thematic strands from the *National Curriculum Standards for Social Studies* through two related classroom activities. The first is Theme 4, **INDIVIDUAL DEVELOPMENT AND IDENTITY**, which addresses personal identity as shaped by family, peers, culture, and institutional influences. From the theme's "Knowledge" goals for the Early Grades, the expectations are that learners will understand "concepts such as: growth, change, learning, self, family, and groups."[1] Theme 5, **INDIVIDUALS, GROUPS, AND INSTITUTIONS**, is also addressed, as stated in that theme's "Purpose": "Institutions such as families...exert great influence in daily life."[2]

The first activity is based on two questions: What Do You Do with Your Home Family? and What Do You Do with Your School Family? The questions are designed to spark an interest in young learners to share what they do with other people, particularly with just one of their parents/guardians as illustrated in the book. By reflecting on their home families and everyday activities, young learners will discover that they are engaged in many different activities with a parent/guardian. As children share their family activities with their peers, the similarities and differences become visible and reveal both unique and matching patterns. Children will begin to negotiate their understanding of their own personal identities and of distinctive characteristics of their peers.

Investigating home families encompasses the first part of this classroom activity. The second part of this classroom activity focuses on contextualizing personal identities and distinctive characteristics by transferring them into the social processes of the school family. Young learners examine classroom and school activities as extensions of their personal interests and group perceptions. Building upon the home family to establish the school family activities demonstrates the increasing roles that young learners must develop and fulfill as they age.

The second activity emphasizes NCSS Theme 9, **GLOBAL CONNECTIONS**, which is evident in the illustrations of child and parent activities from around the world. Global interdependence requires an understanding of connections among individuals, groups, and institutions. The classroom activity for this theme pursues the question: How Are People Alike and Different at Home and School All Around the World? Students can see that some of the same child-parent activities are conducted using different objects, or for different purposes. Young learners start to associate the links shared locally and globally through individual needs and wants. They can begin to understand how global connections affect daily life for individuals and those around them.

Class Activity 1

What Do You Do with Your Home Family?
What Do You Do with Your School Family?

NCSS Curriculum Standards

④ INDIVIDUAL DEVELOPMENT AND IDENTITY

KNOWLEDGE EARLY GRADES
Learners will understand...
▶ Concepts such as: growth, change, learning, self, family, and groups;
▶ Individuals have characteristics that are both distinct from and similar to those of others.

⑤ INDIVIDUALS, GROUPS AND INSTITUTIONS

KNOWLEDGE EARLY GRADES
Learners will understand...
▶ Concepts such as: community, culture, role, competition, cooperation, rules, and norms;
▶ The impact of families [and] schools ... on their lives.

National Curriculum Standards for Social Studies, pp. 39, 43.

Procedures

▶ After reading the book aloud and talking about the lyrical pattern of words in the text, give each student a disposable camera to take home with the directions that three photographs should be taken showing the child with one parent/guardian engaged in three favorite everyday activities. If cameras are not available, then provide each student with three sheets of construction paper on which the learner draws three different illustrations of himself or herself with at least one parent together engaged in everyday home activities. The construction paper should be cut in the dimensions to fit into the pockets of a large pocket chart.

▶ Develop the photographs and glue them to individual sheets of construction paper.

▶ Assist learners in writing a phrase below each photograph or drawing, using the same pattern found in the text with an action word ending with *–ing* followed by an object word.

▶ Display large pocket charts where the children can access them easily. Place each photograph or drawing into one of the pocket charts grouped with phrases starting with the same or similar *–ing* action words.

▶ Guide the children to select groups of the photographs or drawings that show the various activities associated with a particular *–ing* action word, such as *walking home, walking the dog, walking through a field*.

▶ Repeat the assignment at school with either cameras or drawings that depict three favorite everyday school activities.

▶ Again, write the phrases that describe the activities, and group them in the pocket charts.

▶ To extend the activities and increase critical thinking, ask the learners to generate more *–ing* action words and object words.

▶ Bind the photographs or drawings together into big books for children to share with families, either at school during an open house or at parent-teacher conferences, and finally to take home in their book baskets.

▶ To integrate these activities, read aloud other books from the book lists.

▶ Lead the class in singing the song: "This Is My School Family," recorded by Jack Hartman from the CD "It Starts in the Heart" by Becky Bailey and Jack Hartman at www.songsforteaching. com/store/it-starts-in-the-heart-cd-jack-hartmann-dr-becky-bailey-pr-1432.html

How Are People Alike and Different at Home and School All Around the World?

NCSS Curriculum Standards

❹ INDIVIDUAL DEVELOPMENT AND IDENTITY

❾ GLOBAL CONNECTIONS

QUESTION FOR EXPLORATION EARLY GRADES

▶ How do children in other parts of the world grow and learn?

KNOWLEDGE EARLY GRADES
Learners will understand…

▶ Global connections affect daily life for individuals and those around them.

National Curriculum Standards for Social Studies, pp. 38, 59.

Procedures

1. To begin this lesson, cut four identical large circles using bulletin board background paper. Each circle should be approximately three feet in diameter with one circle in light green, one circle in light blue, one circle in light yellow, and one circle in light purple. Stack the four circles together, and cut out medium-sized, simple shaped puzzle pieces all at one time, so that all four circles are cut into identical puzzle pieces. The circles should be cut into enough puzzle pieces for each learner to have an individual piece. The puzzle pieces should be large enough for learners to draw individual pictures on each puzzle piece. For example, if there are 25 learners, you will have 25 light green, light blue, light yellow and light purple puzzle pieces.

2. Using similar bulletin board background paper in light green, light blue, light yellow, and light purple, cut four large question marks approximately three feet tall. Stack the four question marks together and cut medium-sized, simple shaped puzzle pieces all at one time, so that all four question marks are cut into identical puzzle pieces. The question marks should be cut into enough puzzle pieces for each learner to have an individual piece. The puzzle pieces should be large enough for learners to write individual words on each puzzle piece. For example, if there are 25 learners, you will have 25 light green, light blue, light yellow and light purple puzzle pieces.

3. Start with the circle puzzle pieces in light green. Give each learner a puzzle piece and ask the learner to draw himself or herself engaged in an activity with just one adult at school, building upon the ideas and photographs from the book *You and Me Together*. After the drawings are completed, assemble the puzzle pieces, showing how all the pieces fit together to form the world of school. Do not glue the puzzle pieces permanently as the puzzle pieces will be used again.

4. Lead a conversation noting how people are both alike and different from one another in their activities at school.

5. Now give each learner a question mark puzzle piece in light green. Ask each learner to write the *–ing* action word shown in her or his light green puzzle piece. Assemble the large light green question mark puzzle pieces and lead a conversation related to the actions at school.

6. Give each learner the same shaped puzzle piece cut from the blue paper circle to take home with the directions to draw a picture of himself or herself engaged in an activity with just one parent or guardian at home. Learners should return their puzzle pieces to school the next day.

7. As a class, assemble the puzzle pieces, showing how all pieces fit together, accompanied by a conversation noting similarities and differences at home compared and contrasted with activities at school.

8. Now give each learner the matching question mark puzzle piece in light blue. Ask each learner to write the –ing action word shown in the light blue question mark puzzle piece. Assemble the large light blue question mark and lead a conversation related to the actions at home.

9. Arrange for one set of pen pals the same age from another country. Use the website "Learners of the World" at www.learnersoftheworld.info/menu_pres.html to connect with international teachers. Send a copy of *You and Me Together* and two sets of circle puzzle pieces: one in light yellow paper and one in light purple paper with directions for the learners to draw pictures of themselves engaged in an activity with just one adult at school on the yellow puzzle pieces and engaged in an activity with just one adult at home on the purple puzzle pieces. Provide stamps and addressed envelopes for students to return their puzzle pieces.

10. When the two sets of puzzle pieces are returned, assemble the puzzles into two circles showing activities at school and activities at home.

11. Now give each learner the matching question mark puzzle piece in light yellow. Ask each learner to write the –ing action word shown in the pen pal's corresponding light yellow circle puzzle piece. Assemble the large light yellow question mark and lead a conversation related to the actions at the pen pal's school.

12. Then give each learner the matching question mark puzzle piece in light purple. Ask each learner to write the –ing action word shown in the pen pal's corresponding light purple circle puzzle piece. Assemble the large light purple question mark and lead a conversation related to the actions at the pen pal's home.

13. Place the pieces from all four circle puzzles and scramble the pieces together. Ask each learner to select a puzzle piece and assemble four new puzzles using puzzle pieces that combine green, blue, yellow, and purple puzzle pieces. Lead the learners in a conversation emphasizing the global interdependence between the two sets of learners.

14. Repeat step 12 with the pieces from all four question mark puzzles emphasizing the –ing action words found locally and globally. Teachers can connect this conversation to world sports to maintain the interest of students.

15. Lead the class in singing the song "Places in the World," by Red and Kathy Grammer, which can be found at www.n-e-n.com/redgrammer-teaching-peacesongbook.aspx

16. Other activities related to global studies can be found on the CD "Teaching Peace," a Shirley Handy Publication with the Singing-Reading Connection Series.

17. Share more selections of children's literature to highlight geographic locations around the world and the internationally shared joys of childhood.

18. As learners experience new ideas and vocabulary, refer to the circle and question mark puzzles and practice associating –ing action words with various objects, people, and places.

Reading Activities

These activities can help to meet the following Reading Standards for Literature from the Common Core State Standards for English Language Arts:

READING: LITERATURE-KINDERGARTEN
(There are no standards for Pre-K)
Key Ideas and Details
  1. With prompting and support, ask and answer questions about key details in a text.
Craft and Structure
  4. Ask and answer questions about unknown words in a text.
Range of Reading and Level of Text Complicity
  10. Actively engage in group reading activities with purpose and understanding.

Common Core State Standards for English Language Arts and Literacy in History/Social Studies, Science, and Technical Subjects, p. 11.

KWHL (Know, What, How, Learned)

As a pre-assessment to measure learners' prior knowledge and to motivate interest, conduct a KWHL before starting any of the lessons. Tell the learners that they are going to read a book about moms, dads, and kids around the world. To explore "what they **K**now," ask the learners about the kinds of everyday activities they do with either their moms or dads (guardians, grandparents, etc). List the responses on a large sheet of colorful paper and read the words aloud to the children.

Showing the cover of the book *You and Me Together: Moms, Dads, and Kids Around the World,* investigate "what the learners **W**ant to know," by asking them to predict what the text is about. Show them illustrations they might find inside the book. List the responses on a second large sheet of colorful paper in a different color and read the words aloud to the class.

As you read each paper and show the illustrations, ask the children to describe the photographs and the people shown in each photo, e.g., their clothing, their surroundings, and their activities. As students contribute to the conversation, prompt them to "explain **H**ow they know what they are learning." List their responses on a third sheet of paper.

After the learners complete all of the activities related to this unit of learning, ask them to share "what they have **L**earned" to showcase the vocabulary, concepts, and practices. Record their ideas on a fourth large sheet of colorful paper, and print the children's contributions, using correct spelling and repeating the words and phrases aloud for all learners to repeat and remember.

Vocabulary

Learners will acquire several sets of vocabulary from the text or associated with the text.

▸ To demonstrate their comprehension of verbs related to actions, ask children to act out the *–ing* words (present participles) using various objects to complete the activities.

sharing	**holding**	**catching**
playing	**telling**	**dancing**
taking	**making**	**seeing**

▸ To demonstrate their comprehension of words about things (nouns), ask children to point to the objects represented by the words or to describe the meaning of the words.

you	**nap**	**bus**
me	**pet**	**ball**
we	**rake**	**turn**
joke	**tale**	**sun**
shade	**mess**	**storm**
ride	**meal**	
tune	**fish**	

- To apply their knowledge related to words about place and time (adjectives), have the students use each word in an oral sentence.

life   forever
time   here
together

Word Development

- To account for their understanding related to words about families and various names for each relationship, help the students to incorporate the words in stories.

mother   uncle
father   grandmother
brother   grandfather
sister   child and children
aunt   family

- To exhibit their involvement in various daily activities, guide the students as they perform/act out the verbs, to demonstrate comprehension of action words.

sleeping   singing
eating   smiling
walking   talking
working   listening
playing

- To confirm their awareness related to words about the body, ask the children to show these through action songs.

boy   face
girl   arm
man   hand
woman   leg
head   foot

- To show connections between categories of words and specific objects, engage the children in matching activities at learning centers.

world   plant
land   house
water   clothes
sky   tools
food   toys
animal   games
pets   fun

Other Recommended Books for All Ten of the NCSS Themes in the Prekindergarten/ Kindergarten Classroom

There are no specific Common Core Standards for English Language Arts at the Prekindergarten level. All the following books can be used to meet Standard 1 of the Common Core Reading Standards for Literature at the Kindergarten level: "With prompting and support, ask and answer questions about key details in a text." As teachers review the books, they can use the chart of standards on pp. 8–9 to develop strategies for meeting other Common Core Reading Standards for Literature in Kindergarten when they use the books in class.

❶ CULTURE

Norma Simon, *All Families are Special* (Morton Grove, IL: Albert Whitman & Company, 2003)
Vivid watercolors show a wide range of families in many cultures. The text provides an easy-to-read narrative from the voice of a young learner using vocabulary related to families and the time spent together.
QUESTION FOR EXPLORATION: How does a culture unify a group of people?

❷ TIME, CONTINUITY, AND CHANGE

Karen Ackerman, *Song and Dance Man* (New York: Knopf Books for Young Readers, 2003)

Grandpa dons the clothing from the attic left over from his days as a vaudeville performer to entertain his grandchildren by performing tricks, playing the banjo, and telling jokes. The softly illustrated pictures and gentle text relay the concepts of time passing, aging and nostalgia.

QUESTION FOR EXPLORATION: How do we know about the past?

❸ PEOPLE, PLACES, AND ENVIRONMENTS

Liz Garton Scanlon, *All the World* (New York: Beach Lane Books, 2009)

Told through rhymes, the stories of several families and their daily endeavors are portrayed in various locations with enchanting drawings and rhyming verse in this book, which was a Notable Social Studies Trade Book in 2010. The book expresses contentment with the pleasures of a summer day and celebrates humankind in local and global environments.

QUESTION FOR EXPLORATION: What are the physical and human characteristics of place?

❹ INDIVIDUAL DEVELOPMENT AND IDENTITY

Sheila Hamanaka, *All the Colors of the Earth* (New York: William Morrow, 1994)

As a celebration of all people's heritages, this book is filled with paintings linking the colors of the earth with the descriptions of people's appearances. The simple yet expressive text captures the reader's interest and imagination. This book was a Notable Social Studies Trade Book in 1995.

QUESTION FOR EXPLORATION: How am I different from and similar to others?

❺ INDIVIDUALS, GROUPS, AND INSTITUTIONS

Heather Adamson, *School in Many Cultures: Life Around the World* (Mankato, MN: Capstone Press, Pebble Plus, 2009)

Highlighted with photographs of worldwide schools, this book shows learners attending classes in many different locations around the world. The text is one of a series about cultural universals such as homes, families, and clothing.

QUESTION FOR EXPLORATION: How do civic, educational, governmental, and religious organizations function in our community, state, and nation?

❻ POWER, AUTHORITY, AND GOVERNANCE

Langston Hughes, *My People* (New York: Simon & Schuster, Atheneum, 2009)

The inspirational words from Langston Hughes' 1923 poem celebrate the faces, hearts, souls, and characteristics of humanity. Intelligence, wisdom, curiosity, love and joy are captured in a collection of sepia-colored photographs of African-Americans of all ages. The photographs and poem convey the power of freedom and citizenship for all.

QUESTION FOR EXPLORATION: How is power gained?

❼ PRODUCTION, DISTRIBUTION, AND CONSUMPTION

DK Publishing, *A Life Like Mine* (New York: DK Publishing, 2005)

This book of photographs depicts a typical day for 18 children from 180 countries categorized into four themes: survival, development, protections, and participation. Supporting the United National Convention on the Rights of the Child, the text shows a positive view of life and the opportunities children encounter even in the face of adversity.

QUESTION FOR EXPLORATION: Why can't people have everything that they want?

❽ SCIENCE, TECHNOLOGY, AND SOCIETY

Maya Ajmera, John D. Ivanko, and Fred Rogers, *Be My Neighbor* (Watertown, MA: Charlesbridge Publishing, 2006)

Based on the words of Fred Rogers, brilliantly colorful photographs of neighborhoods from around the world depict parts of communities including homes, schools, religious buildings, shopping districts, recreational areas, transportation, and celebrations.

QUESTION FOR EXPLORATION: What are wants or needs to which science and technology have been applied?

❾ GLOBAL CONNECTIONS

Mem Fox, *Whoever You Are* (New York: Houghton Mifflin Harcourt, 2007)
All children love, smile, laugh, and cry. The illustrations emphasizing color, shape, and texture depict the humanity of life shared by children locally and globally.
QUESTION FOR EXPLORATION: What are the effects of increasing global connections?

❿ CIVIC IDEALS AND PRACTICES

Barbara Kerley, *A Little Peace* (Washington, DC: National Geographic Children's Books, 2007)
Photographs of youngsters from around the world portray simple actions that contribute to peace, such as sharing a smile and making new friends. The book, which was a Notable Social Studies Trade Book in 2008, includes short descriptions of each location and an afterword by Richard Solomon, President of the U.S. Institute of Peace.
QUESTION FOR EXPLORATION: What are key democratic ideals and practices? 🌐

NOTES

1. National Council for the Social Studies (NCSS), *National Curriculum Standards for Social Studies: A Framework for Teaching, Learning, and Assessment* (Silver Spring, MD: NCSS, 2010), 39.

2. *Ibid.*, 42.

The books cited in this chapter are recommended for their value in implementing the National Curriculum Standards for Social Studies and the Common Core State Standards for English Language Arts and Literacy at the Prekindergarten/Kindergarten level. They can also be used to help to meet the following standards of the national Standards for the English Language Arts published in 1996 by the International Reading Association and National Council of Teachers of English.

International Reading Association (IRA) and National Council of Teachers of English (NCTE), *Standards for the English Language Arts* (Newark, DE and Urbana, IL: IRA and NCTE, 1996): 19, 22.

1 Students read a wide range of print and nonprint texts to build an understanding of texts, of themselves, and of the cultures of the United States and the world; to acquire new information; to respond to the needs and demands of society and the workplace; and for personal fulfillment. Among these texts are fiction and nonfiction, classic and contemporary works.
Reading is a wonderfully rich and complex human activity. It provokes reflection, introspection, and imaginative thinking and allows us to create and explore new ideas. It introduces us to different representations of the world. It fills our needs for information and communication and enables us to learn about different subjects, perform various tasks, participate in the workplace, and understand and evaluate our place in the world. It also gives us the intrinsic pleasure of linguistic and imaginative activity.
Even before they enter school, children can learn to enjoy books and other print material....

3 Students apply a wide range of strategies to comprehend, interpret, evaluate, and appreciate texts. They draw on their prior experience, their interactions with other readers and writers, their knowledge of word meaning and of other texts, their word identification strategies, and their understanding of textual features (e.g., sound-letter correspondence, sentence structure, context, graphics)

6 Kindergarten

Syd Golston and Patricia Kennedy

Make Way for Ducklings
Written and illustrated by Robert McCloskey
New York: Viking Press, 1941

This charming volume won the Caldecott Medal as "the most distinguished American picture book for children" in 1941. For 70 years, generations of children have delighted in McCloskey's vivid line drawings of Mr. and Mrs. Mallard and their new ducklings in aerial and street views of Boston and its famed Public Gardens.

Mr. and Mrs. Mallard explore Boston for the perfect site to build their nest. The pond in the Public Gardens seems ideal, because the people in the swan boats feed them peanuts — but it's too busy and dangerous, with children zooming by on their bicycles. After flying over famous city sites, they choose a quiet island to hatch their ducklings and to teach them to swim and dive, come when called, and swim in line. When the Mallards decide to relocate the family to the Public Gardens with those peanut treats, there's a crisis: how can the little line of ducklings navigate busy city streets? Clancy the policeman and his officer friends stop traffic to give them safe passage.

The mallard parents teach and shelter their young, and police officer Clancy takes care of them as well, paralleling the experience small children have as their parents and community members protect and nurture them — age appropriate concepts in NCSS Social

Social Studies Standards Themes
❹ INDIVIDUAL DEVELOPMENT AND IDENTITY
❸ PEOPLE, PLACES AND ENVIRONMENTS
❺ INDIVIDUALS, GROUPS AND INSTITUTIONS

Common Core Standards
READING: LITERATURE—KINDERGARTEN
Key Ideas and Details
1. With prompting and support, ask and answer questions about key details in a text.

Craft and Structure
4. Ask and answer questions about unknown words in a text.

READING: FOUNDATIONAL SKILLS—KINDERGARTEN
Phonological Awareness
2. Demonstrate understanding of spoken words, syllables, and sounds (phonemes)
(a) Recognize and produce rhyming words.

LANGUAGE—KINDERGARTEN
Conventions of Standard English
1. Demonstrate command of the conventions of standard English grammar and usage when writing or speaking….
(b) Use frequently occurring nouns and verbs.
2. Demonstrate command of the conventions of standard English capitalization,…

Vocabulary Acquisition and Use
4. Determine or clarify the meaning of unknown and multiple-meaning words based on *kindergarten reading and content.*

Studies Theme 4, **INDIVIDUAL DEVELOPMENT AND IDENTITY**. This theme comprises Questions for Exploration, Knowledge topics, Processes, and Products that learners encounter in the behavioral sciences (psychology, sociology, anthropology). "In the early grades, young learners develop their personal identities in the context of families, peers, schools, and communities. Central to this development is the exploration, identification, and analysis of how individuals and groups are like and unique as well as how they relate in supportive and collaborative ways."

As the teacher reads *Make Way for Ducklings*, she draws out the parallels between the ducklings and human children. Mr. and Mrs. Mallard protect their offspring as they go through growth stages — eggs, hatchlings, ducklings. The children's parents/guardians do this too, and the teacher can elicit ways in which parents/guardians protect children before they are born, when they are helpless babies, and as they grow into childhood. This is an opportunity to introduce questions and concepts from Theme 4 of the social studies standards, **INDIVIDUAL DEVELOPMENT AND IDENTITY**. Questions for that theme include: "How am I changing in physical and personal development over time? How have others influenced who I am and who I am becoming?"[1] A knowledge expectation is that learners will understand "key concepts such as growth, change, learning, self, family, groups."[2]

Children in kindergarten are aware that they are growing and changing, just as the ducklings were when they got their flying feathers – the children are getting taller, losing baby teeth, outgrowing their clothes and shoes. One of the "Products" suggested in Theme 4, "Drawing two pictures of themselves to describe how they have changed during the year," could be used.[3]

Some knowledge of NCSS Curriculum Standard Theme 3, **PEOPLE, PLACES, AND ENVIRONMENTS** may also be taught through the book. *Make Way for Ducklings* is one of the files at **www.googlelitinfo.com**, a Google site which uses GPS software to show the locales mentioned in well-known K-12 books. Teachers can show students the Public Garden with its swan boats, Beacon Hill, Louisburg Square, Mount Vernon Street and the Corner Book Shop, all at street level. The teacher can also introduce the geographic features of the "pond," "island" and "river bank."

Two extended social studies activities for the book return us to the **INDIVIDUAL DEVELOPMENT AND IDENTITY** theme. The first, hatching chicks (or ducklings, although they are harder to obtain) in the classroom combines science and social studies in an intensive experience which students find thrilling and memorable. The book is the perfect kickoff for such an extended activity. The connections to human growth and development, parental care and social learning, may be made throughout. Students can even vote to name the hatchlings — another piece of civic learning.

The second activity, a guest speaker visit by a police officer, is also a favorite for the children. Clancy, the Boston policeman in the book, embodies the "community helpers" popular in the kindergarten curriculum. Police departments throughout the country have developed speaker programs for the youngest of young learners, generally emphasizing the kinder and gentler safety topics characterized by Clancy and his fellow officers.

Pre-reading practice suggestions provided are in the areas of Prediction, Vocabulary, Phonemic Awareness, Capitalization, Words with Multiple Meanings, and Verb Practice. The word lists included here can be made into colorful handouts with the aid of *Make Way for Ducklings* clip art, available at Google Images.

Finally, we recommend nine Kindergarten books covering the rest of the Ten Themes, which are briefly annotated at the end of the chapter.

Raising Chicks or Ducklings in the Kindergarten Classroom

NCSS Curriculum Standard

❹ INDIVIDUAL DEVELOPMENT AND IDENTITY

KNOWLEDGE EARLY GRADES

Learners will understand...

▸ Concepts such as: growth, change, learning, self, family, and groups;

▸ Individuals have characteristics that are both distinct from and similar to those of others.

National Curriculum Standards for Social Studies, p. 39

Procedures

▸ Contact a local farm or park to obtain eggs.

▸ Purchase a chick incubator (sources: Delta Science Company or a local feed store). You want one with an automatic egg turner.

DISCUSSION QUESTION: How did Mrs. Mallard provide a natural duckling incubator for her babies? (Building a nest away from dangers to the eggs, sitting on the eggs to keep them warm)

▸ Arrange for the eggs to be delivered in the middle of the week – they take 21 days exactly – you want the children to see the hatchings.

▸ Crack open a grocery egg to show the membrane and the pores, the air space, the food and water supply for the chick.

▸ Use "Chick Life Cycle Exploration Set" to show the children what's happening on each of the 21 days before the hatchings. These are 21 plastic eggs containing models of the day to day development of the chick. (Learning Resources, 800-333-8281)

▸ Discuss daily how the chicks are protected in the incubator, and how this parallels how their own parents protected the kindergarten children as they were being "incubated" inside their mothers.

DISCUSSION ASSIGNMENT: Ask your mother how she made sure that you would be healthy before you were born. (Eating well, drinking milk, taking vitamins, resting, etc.)

▸ As the chicks hatch, let the children notice differences among them in color and size. They will be surprised that the chicks aren't all yellow.

DISCUSSION QUESTION: How are the chicks the same? How are they different? How is this true of human babies and children?

▸ Buy Chick Starter feed at a feed store for the chicks after they hatch.

DISCUSSION QUESTION: Did your parents have to buy or make special food for you when you were little? (Formula, baby food because you had no teeth, etc.)

▸ Ask the students to suggest names for each chick as it is born, and hold an election to name each one. DISCUSSION: majority rule.

▸ Keep the chicks in the incubator for 24 hours until their feathers dry, and then move them to a brooder box (plastic tub or cardboard box), with a lamp above it for heat.

▸ In about two weeks, the chicks will develop flight feathers, and you will have to find a home outside the classroom for them.

Mrs. Mallard and her ducklings in bronze, in the Boston Public Garden today.

A Classroom Visit from a Police Officer

NCSS Curriculum Standard

❹ INDIVIDUAL DEVELOPMENT AND IDENTITY

QUESTIONS FOR EXPLORATION EARLY GRADES

How can institutions help to meet individual needs and promote the common good?

KNOWLEDGE EARLY GRADES

Learners will understand...

▸ People's interactions with their social and physical surroundings influence individual identity and growth.

❺ INDIVIDUALS, GROUPS, AND INSTITUTIONS

KNOWLEDGE EARLY GRADES

Learners will understand...

▸ The impact of... government agencies... on their lives.

National Curriculum Standards for Social Studies, pp. 38, 39, 43.

The character of Clancy, the police officer who guides the ducklings to safety in busy Boston traffic, provides the impetus for a popular Kindergarten event: the visit of a police officer as a guest speaker. In a discussion which accompanies *Make Way for Ducklings* about people who protect us, children themselves will bring up police officers who keep the streets safe for them, and ward off the "bad guys."

The teacher begins a simple drawing exercise that focuses the children on police officers: what they wear, what they drive, where they work, what they do (which could include some sophisticated ideas from television). After the class drawings are finished and posted, the teacher shows, on a simple map, where the nearest police station is located. The class can make a vocabulary list of words like uniform, traffic, squad car, siren, badge, arrest. This is also the time to read through pamphlets that some departments offer to elementary students.

The students should then put together a list of questions for the police officer. It's best not to edit questions, even those that seem silly, because the

officers who are experienced with young learners are delighted by these and quite adept at turning them into teachable moments. For instance, if a student wants to know whether the officer ever stopped cars for a family of ducklings, he or she can turn the question into other ways that the police protect animals by enforcing leash laws and traffic regulations. Officers are experienced in deflecting discussions of violence, should the use of their guns come up.

Police officers usually prepare their own program, which may or may not match the children's questions; they deal with topics like bicycle safety, seat belt use, stranger danger, and bullying. After the formal presentation, young learners can ask the questions each of them posed. The final and often most exciting part of the visit is a trip to the parking lot to see the motorcycle or squad car.

After the officer leaves, children should assist the teacher in writing and signing their names on a thank you note to their guest.

Reading Activities

These activities can help to meet the following Reading and Language Standards from the Common Core State Standards for English Language Arts (Kindergarten).

READING: LITERATURE—KINDERGARTEN
Key Ideas and Details
1. With prompting and support, ask and answer questions about key details in a text.

Craft and Structure
4. Ask and answer questions about unknown words in a text.

READING: FOUNDATIONAL SKILLS—KINDERGARTEN
Phonological Awareness
2. Demonstrate understanding of spoken words, syllables, and sounds (phonemes)
(a) Recognize and produce rhyming words.

LANGUAGE—KINDERGARTEN
Conventions of Standard English
1. Demonstrate command of the conventions of standard English grammar and usage when writing or speaking….
(b) Use frequently occurring nouns and verbs.

2. Demonstrate command of the conventions of standard English capitalization,…

Vocabulary Acquisition and Use
4. Determine or clarify the meaning of unknown and multiple-meaning words based on *kindergarten reading and content.*

Common Core Standards for English Language Arts and Literacy in History/Social Studies, Science, and Technical Subjects, p. 11 (Reading Literature); p. 15 (Foundational Skills); p. 26 (Language).

Prediction

Ask the children, after showing them the cover of the book: What will be happening in the book *Make Way for Ducklings?*

Several times, before you turn the page to the next one, ask: What will happen next? (Example: what happens after Mrs. Mallard lays the eggs and sits on them?)

Vocabulary

▸ Assign the students 12 key words from the book:

mallard	dither	public	island
waddle	molt	proud	hatch
squawk	responsibility	opposite	bank

▸ Lead practice aloud in putting the new verbs in past tense:
waddled, squawked, molted, hatched

Phonemic Awareness

▸ Ask the children to notice the alphabetical duckling names, and then they can imagine that there are not just eight but ten ducklings; after Jack, Kack, Lack, Mack, Nack, Ouack, Pack, and Quack, they name Rack and Sack.

▸ The Mallards could decide to name all eight ducklings with "M" names. Tell the students to choose the M names from pairs that include rhyming nouns that do not begin with M:

Mack, Sack	**Mud, Bud**
Milk, Silk	**Mike, Bike**
Monday, Sunday	**May, Bay**
Mop, Top	**Moon, Noon**

Capitalization

▸ Show the children that proper names of specific places are capitalized: Boston, Public Garden, Beacon Hill, State House, Louisburg Square, Charles River, Mount Vernon Street, and Corner Book Shop. This might be a time to use the *Make Way for Ducklings* file at www.googlelitinfo.com, which takes the students to these sites.

▸ Help students to capitalize the names of their own city or town, nearby rivers, streets, parks, or stores.

▸ Remind them that names are also capitalized: Mr. and Mrs. Mallard, Clancy.

Words with More than One Meaning

▶ Point out words in Make Way for Ducklings that have two or more meanings:

raise a family   *spend* the night   river *bank*
the Mallards *called* on Michael
he *planted* himself in the center of the road

▶ Follow up practice could include a wall chart for displaying such words as they turn up in children's reading over the semester or the year.

Verb Practice

▶ Mrs. Mallard taught her ducklings to:

Swim   Dive   Walk in line
Come when called
Keep a safe distance from things with wheels

▶ Ask the children to make a verb list of their parents' or their teacher's instructions for them, and act them out: share, brush your teeth, eat your dinner, etc. — and the last two (come when called, keep a safe distance from things with wheels) could be the same.

Other Recommended Books for the Kindergarten Classroom

These books can be used to teach the nine social studies standards themes other than Theme 4, **INDIVIDUAL DEVELOPMENT AND IDENTITY**, which is the main focus of Activity 1 above. All of the books can be used to meet Standard 1 of the Common Core Reading Standards for Literature for Kindergarten: "With prompting and support, ask and answer questions about key details in the text." As teachers review the books, they can use the chart of standards on pp. 8–9 to develop strategies for meeting other Common Core Reading Standards for Literature in Kindergarten when they use the books in class.

❶ CULTURE

Eric Kimmel, *Hershel and the Hanukkah Goblins* (New York: Holiday House, 1994)
Hershel protects the villagers' traditions of Hanukkah (candles, dreidels, potato pancakes) in this fanciful story.
QUESTION FOR EXPLORATION: How do the beliefs, values, and behaviors of a group of people help the group meet its needs and solve problems?

❷ TIME, CONTINUITY, AND CHANGE

Mem Fox, *Wilfred Gordon McDonald Partridge* (New York: Kane/Miller Books, 1989)
Little Wilfred learns the concepts of "long ago," time, and memory through his friends in the nursing home next door.
QUESTION FOR EXPLORATION: How do we know about the past?

❸ PEOPLE, PLACES, AND ENVIRONMENTS

Joan Sweeney and Annette Cable, *Me on the Map* (New York: Dragonfly Books, 1998)
A little girl maps her room, then her house, the street, the neighborhood, city, state, and country, in a book that provides the blueprint for a beginning geography unit for children.
QUESTION FOR EXPLORATION: How do simple geographic skills and tools help humans understand spatial relationships?

❺ INDIVIDUALS, GROUPS, AND INSTITUTIONS

Daniel Pinkwater, *The Big Orange Splot* (New York: Scholastic, 1993)
The pressure of his neighbors can't make Mr. Plumbean change his individuality – their houses all look the same, until the creative color scheme of Plumbean's home inspires them to express individual creativity in house paints.
QUESTION FOR EXPLORATION: How am I different from and similar to others?

⑥ POWER, AUTHORITY, AND GOVERNANCE

Doreen Cronin, *Click, Clack, Moo* (New York: Simon & Schuster Children's Publishing, 2000)

Farmer Brown's cows use collective power to stage a strike against him. They refuse to give milk until Farmer Brown provides blankets for them in the cold barn.

QUESTION FOR EXPLORATION: How is power gained?

⑦ PRODUCTION, DISTRIBUTION, AND CONSUMPTION

Judith Viorst, *Alexander Who Used to Be Rich Last Sunday* (New York: Atheneum, 1987)

Grandparents give three young brothers a dollar apiece. Anthony and Nicholas save their money, while Alexander squanders his — a lesson in thrift for little ones.

QUESTION FOR EXPLORATION: Why can't people have everything they want?

⑧ SCIENCE, TECHNOLOGY, AND SOCIETY

Monica Kulling, *Eat My Dust! Henry Ford's First Race* (New York: Random House, 2004)

Henry Ford enters a car race to earn prize money so that he can start a factory to make affordable automobiles for everyone. The story is based on historical events.

QUESTION FOR EXPLORATION: How can science and technology be used to address individual, social, and global problems or issues?

⑨ GLOBAL CONNECTIONS

Reeve Lindbergh, *Our Nest* (Somerville, MA: Candlewick, 2004)

All of Earth's denizens are interrelated — the child in his or her bed, fish in brooks, boats in their harbors, stars in the nest of space.

QUESTION FOR EXPLORATION: How are people, places, and environments connected around the globe?

⑩ CIVIC IDEALS AND PRACTICES

Eleanor Batezat Sisulu, *The Day Gogo Went To Vote* (Boston: Little, Brown, 1999)

Gogo is a 100 year old great-grandmother who is determined to vote for the first time in her life. Little Thembi goes with her to the polling place in the first free multi-racial election in South Africa in 1994.

QUESTION FOR EXPLORATION: What are civic practices? 📚

NOTES

1. National Council for the Social Studies (NCSS), *National Curriculum Standards for Social Studies: A Framework for Teaching, Learning, and Assessment* (Silver Spring, MD: NCSS, 2010), 38.

2. *Ibid*, 39.

3. *Ibid*, 41.

The books cited in this chapter are recommended for their value in implementing the National Curriculum Standards for Social Studies and the Common Core State Standards for English Language Arts at the Kindergarten level. They can also be used to help to meet the following standard of the national Standards for the English Language Arts published in 1996 by the International Reading Association and National Council of Teachers of English.

1 Students read a wide range of print and nonprint texts to build an understanding of texts, of themselves, and of the cultures of the United States and the world; to acquire new information; to respond to the needs and demands of society and the workplace; and for personal fulfillment. Among these texts are fiction and nonfiction, classic and contemporary works.

International Reading Association (IRA) and National Council of Teachers of English (NCTE), *Standards for the English Language Arts* (Newark, DE and Urbana, IL: IRA and NCTE, 1996): 19.

7 First Grade

Elizabeth R. Hinde

Nina Bonita
Written by Ana Maria Machado
Translated by Elena Iribarren
Illustrated by Rosana Faría

San Diego: Kane/Miller (www.kanemiller.com), 1996. Kane/Miller is owned by EDC Publishing, Tulsa, OK, which distributes *Nina Bonita* (1-800-475-4522).

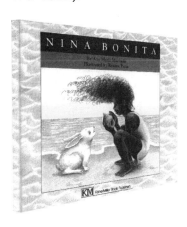

Nina Bonita is an enchanting story that was first published in Brazil and then Venezuela before making its way to the United States in the 1990s. The color-penciled illustrations add to the richness of the story about a white rabbit who is entranced by the distinctive and beautiful dark skin of a young girl, Nina Bonita, in their coastal South American town.

The author's use of figurative language throughout the story, along with the beautiful illustrations, brings the story to life for young readers.

The bunny, "a white rabbit with pink ears, deep red eyes and a quivering nose," lives next door to Nina Bonita and longs to understand why she is the only one in her family who has such dark, beautiful skin. Three times he asks her how she came to be so dark and so pretty because he wants to be as beautiful as she is. Each time, Nina Bonita replies with quite comical and inadequate answers. For instance, Nina Bonita once tells him that she is so dark because black ink was spilled on her as a baby. The rabbit then proceeds to pour black ink all over himself, only to be disappointed when the ink washes away in a rainstorm. Another time, Nina Bonita explains that she ate a great deal of blackberries when she was a baby. So, the rabbit eats a basket of blackberries, only to get a stomachache and take many trips to the bathroom. Finally, the rabbit receives a truthful explanation from Nina Bonita's mother: Nina Bonita is the same color as her black grandmother.

Satisfied with this answer, the rabbit realizes that he cannot become like Nina Bonita, but if he wants to have a daughter as dark and beautiful as Nina Bonita, he will have to marry the right rabbit. Before long he meets and marries a black rabbit and ends up with a plethora of baby rabbits of various hues. The story ends with Nina and the rabbit and his whole multi-colored family living happily ever after.

Social Studies Standards Themes
❶ CULTURE
❸ PEOPLE, PLACES, AND ENVIRONMENTS

Common Core Standards
READING: LITERATURE—GRADE 1
Key Ideas and Details
1. Ask and answer questions about key details in a text.
2. Retell stories, including key details, and demonstrate understanding of their central message or lesson.
3. Describe characters, settings, and major events in a story, using key details.

Integration of Knowledge and Ideas
7. Use illustrations and details in a story to describe its characters, setting, or events.

Throughout the story, the rabbit humorously struggles with coming to an understanding of diversity within his own neighborhood – a concept addressed in Theme 1, **CULTURE**, of the national social studies standards. In an age-appropriate manner, *Nina Bonita* addresses likenesses and differences in people, answering a Key Question for Exploration, "How are groups of people alike and different?"[1] At the same time, students are introduced to some of the traditional and cultural aspects of the village and surrounding areas of Nina Bonita's neighborhood in coastal South America. Learning about the setting of the story addresses the Knowledge section of Theme 1 that states: "culture refers to the behaviors, values, traditions, institutions, and ways of living together of a group of people."[2]

Nina Bonita can also help teachers draw parallels to their students' own experiences with diversity. The story can help students understand that other students and people in their community may be the same or different from themselves in various ways, and that the differences have reasonable and respectable explanations. The teacher can also guide students in age-appropriate discussions about their own experiences with or observations of intolerance because of skin color. Discussion of skin color and intolerance is an example of a Process suggested for Theme 1, **CULTURE**, in the national social studies standards: "Demonstrate how holding different values and beliefs can contribute or pose obstacles to understanding between people and groups."[3]

Learning about the setting also addresses Theme 3, **PEOPLE, PLACES, AND ENVIRONMENTS**. Through the illustrations and storyline, readers travel with the rabbit to the shore, houses, parks, and other places in and around the village. Students will be introduced to core geographic concepts of location and physical and human characteristics, concepts included in the Knowledge expectations of this theme of the standards.

Two activities included in this chapter help students learn about diversity around them and how the physical environment influences culture and social conditions, both concepts from the Knowledge expectations for the early grades. The first activity has students identify similarities and differences among themselves through the use of simple interviews and a Venn diagram. The second activity relates directly to the book by having students draw rudimentary maps of the places the rabbit visited in the story. This activity reinforces comprehension while demonstrating the influence of the physical environment on culture.

Reading suggestions for this book cover Prediction, Vocabulary, Comprehension, and Figurative Language. The Prediction and Vocabulary activities will also be useful for working with English Language Learners.

Finally, at the end of this chapter, nine books for first graders are listed that address social studies themes other than that dealing with Theme 1, **CULTURE** (which is featured in the main activity presented in this chapter). Brief descriptions of each book are also included with each entry.

Similarities and Differences

NCSS Curriculum Standard

❶ CULTURE

QUESTION FOR EXPLORATION EARLY GRADES

▶ How are groups of people alike and different?

KNOWLEDGE EARLY GRADES

Learners will understand...

▶ "Culture" refers to the behaviors, beliefs, values, traditions, institutions, and ways of living together of a group of people;

▶ Concepts such as: similarities, differences, beliefs, values, cohesion, and diversity.

PROCESSES EARLY GRADES

Learners will be able to...

▶ Describe the value of both cultural unity and diversity within and across groups;

▶ Demonstrate how holding different values and beliefs can contribute or pose obstacles to understanding between people and groups.

National Curriculum Standards for Social Studies, pp. 26, 27, 28

Procedures

1. Begin a discussion of the likenesses and differences in skin colors of characters in the book. Point out that Nina Bonita has the darkest skin of any character in the book (except for the baby bunnies at the end of the story). She is also darker than the rest of the people in her family.

2. Have students point out other likenesses and differences among the characters in the book.

3. Tape two hula-hoops to the front board or draw two huge circles, making sure that the circles intersect, creating a visual and hands-on Venn diagram. Label one circle "Nina Bonita" and the other circle "Rabbit." Write Nina Bonita's characteristics in the Nina Bonita circle and the rabbit's characteristics in the Rabbit circle. Write characteristics shared by both in the middle of the diagram where the circles intersect (Figure 1).

Figure 1

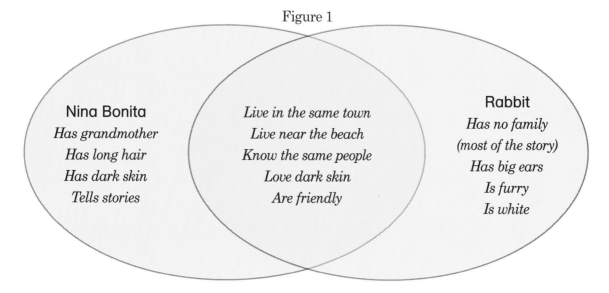

Nina Bonita
Has grandmother
Has long hair
Has dark skin
Tells stories

Live in the same town
Live near the beach
Know the same people
Love dark skin
Are friendly

Rabbit
Has no family
(most of the story)
Has big ears
Is furry
Is white

Figure 2

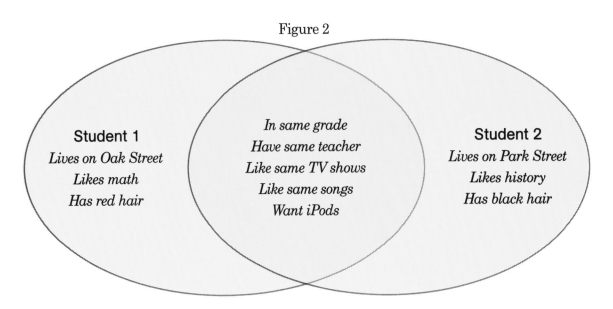

Student 1
Lives on Oak Street
Likes math
Has red hair

In same grade
Have same teacher
Like same TV shows
Like same songs
Want iPods

Student 2
Lives on Park Street
Likes history
Has black hair

4. Repeat this exercise, emphasizing similarities and differences in height, hair color and length, eye color, skin color/freckles, teeth lost, etc. among students in the classroom. (Note: please be diligent in making sure that hurtful, prejudicial, or inappropriate comments are not used in this or other parts of the lesson. The use of language that is a sign of intolerance may indicate the need for another lesson on intolerance or racism.)

5. Organize students into pairs and provide each pair with sticky notes. Draw a Venn diagram (Figure 2) on the board for each pair, or provide a paper copy. (If there are 10 pairs, then draw 10 diagrams.)

6. Have pairs discuss how each of them is the same and how each is different. They should write their unique characteristics on separate sticky notes and how they are alike on other sticky notes. For instance, a characteristic might be that one student has brown hair and the other has blond hair – that would be two notes, one for each circle. A likeness might be that they are both in 1st Grade—that would be one note for the area of the diagram in which the circles overlap. They should also include values and beliefs they both share or

in which they differ as well. They could include such thoughts as: how they feel about certain school or classroom rules, their opinions about what time bedtime should be, or whether or not they think it is OK that Nina Bonita lied to the rabbit throughout the story.

7. Have students label one of the Venn diagrams with their own and their partner's name above each circle. They should place the notes in the appropriate location in the Venn diagram.

8. When all students have completed their diagrams, discuss the likenesses and differences that are noted. Take time discussing the ways all the students are alike – the notes in the middle of each diagram. Point out the many differences, and discuss the importance of working together and being a community even though there are many differences among classmates as well. It is important to understand our differences in order to be a strong community of first graders.

9. Wrap up the lesson by pointing out that we have many things in common and we have many differences, just like the community and the world around us.

Class Activity 2

Mapping the Story

Adapted from an Arizona Geographic Alliance GeoLiteracy lesson by Mimi Norton

NCSS Curriculum Standard

❸ PEOPLE, PLACES, AND ENVIRONMENTS

QUESTIONS FOR EXPLORATION EARLY GRADES

▸ How do simple geographic skills and tools help humans understand spatial relationships?

KNOWLEDGE EARLY GRADES

Learners will understand…

▸ Concepts such as: location, direction, distance and scale;
▸ Tools such as maps…in investigating the relationships among people, places, and environments.

National Curriculum Standards for Social Studies, pp. 34, 35.

Procedures

1. Revisiting the book, have students try to remember all the locations the rabbit visited in the story in order: the beach, Nina's house, the house next to Nina's, the street in town, the town square, etc. List them on chart paper.
2. Explain to students that they are going to draw a map of all the places that the rabbit visited in the story.
3. Distribute drawing paper and colored pencils. Allow students to work in pairs.
4. Students should start by drawing a symbol (or other representation) for the beach where the story starts. Then they should draw a symbol for the house next to Nina's, which is the second place the rabbit visited. They should draw a line from the beach to the house indicating the rabbit's travels.

The next location in the story is Nina's house, so students should draw a symbol for her house and line from the house next to Nina's to Nina's house. After Nina's house, the rabbit returned to the beach, so students should draw a line back to the beach. Follow this procedure until the end of the story. If students are challenged with the task of creating symbols, this could be done as a class with the aim of creating a key listing the symbols (e.g., for the beach, the house, and trees) and recorded on the chart.

5. When the maps are completed, have students retell Nina Bonita through the use of their maps.
6. Post maps in the classroom. Allow students to do a gallery walk to see how other pairs drew their maps.

Reading Activities

These activities can help to meet the following Reading Standards for Literature from the Common Core State Standards for English Language Arts (Grade 1):

READING: LITERATURE—GRADE 1

Key Ideas and Details
1. Ask and answer questions about key details in a text.
2. Retell stories, including key details, and demonstrate understanding of their central message or lesson.
3. Describe characters, settings, and major events in a story, using key details.

Integration of Knowledge and Ideas
7. Use illustrations and details in a story to describe its characters, setting, or events.

Common Core State Standards for English Language Arts and Literacy in History/Social Studies, Science, and Technical Subjects, p. 11.

Prediction

▶ Looking at the cover and thumbing through the pictures, ask students what they think this book is about.

▶ Ask students who or what they think Nina Bonita is. (She and the rabbit are featured prominently on the cover.)

▶ Ask students where they think this story takes place. Point out that the story came from a country in South America called Brazil. (Locate Brazil on a map and/or globe and show the state in which the student's classroom is in relation to the location of Brazil.)

Vocabulary

▶ Students should become familiar with the following words:

Continent	Black olives
South America	Panther
Beach	Fairy
Relatives	Blackberry
Kingdom	

▶ After reading the story, students should show how these words are used in the story.

Comprehension of the Story

▶ Students should use the maps they created in the second activity and retell the story of Nina Bonita.

▶ Using the maps that they created, students should pose two or three questions about the story that include key details regarding the setting or characters. Students should then answer each other's questions. The teacher should ensure that the questions are appropriate.

▶ Using only the pictures in the book, have students describe the events that the pictures describe.

Figurative Language

▶ As the story is being read, point out the use of figurative language. With the students, the teacher should interpret the meaning of the following phrases:
"Her eyes were like two shiny black olives."
"Her hair was curly and pitch black, as if made of unwoven threads of the night."
"Just like a princess."

▶ After reading the story, have students make up other phrases using figurative language to describe themselves. They should create a phrase and then interpret it.

Other Recommended Books for the First Grade Classroom

These books can be used to teach the nine social studies themes other than Theme 1, **CULTURE** (which is in the main focus of Activity 1, above). All of the books can be used to meet Standard 1 of the Common Core Reading Standards for Literature for Grade 1: "Ask and answer questions about key details in a text." As teachers review the books, they can use the chart of standards on pp. 8–9 to develop strategies for meeting other Common Core Reading Standards for Literature in Grade 1 when they use the books in class.

❷ TIME, CONTINUITY, AND CHANGE

Lisa Schnebly Heidinger, *The Three Sedonas* (Phoenix, AZ: Arizona Highways Books, 2000)
This engaging and beautifully illustrated story recounts the life and times of a girl named Sedona and the town in Arizona that was named after her. Narrated by the six-year-old great-great-granddaughter of Sedona Schnebly, the story demonstrates change over time from the perspective of a six-year-old.
QUESTION FOR EXPLORATION: What are the consequences of past events for the present and future?

❸ PEOPLE, PLACES, AND ENVIRONMENTS

Cynthia Rylant and Lisa Desimini, *Tulip Sees America* (New York: Scholastic, 2002)
A young man ventures across America with his dog, Tulip. Readers see America from Nebraska to Oregon from the view of the open road and the driver who is leaving home for the first time.
QUESTION FOR EXPLORATION: What are similarities and differences between places near and far?

❹ INDIVIDUAL DEVELOPMENT AND IDENTITY

Leo Lionni, *A Color of His Own* (New York: Alfred A. Knopf, Dragonfly, 1997)
A chameleon who is unhappy with his own changing appearance befriends another chameleon. Through companionship, the chameleon finds inner peace and satisfaction with his appearance.
QUESTION FOR EXPLORATION: How have others influenced who I am and who I am becoming?

❺ INDIVIDUALS, GROUPS, AND INSTITUTIONS

Alice McLerran, *Roxaboxen* (New York: HarperCollins, 1991)
A group of young children create an imaginary town complete with a mayor, town hall, shops, and even a cemetery in a field near their homes.
QUESTION FOR EXPLORATION: How do the groups to which I belong influence me, and how do I influence them?

❻ POWER, AUTHORITY, AND GOVERNANCE

David Catrow, *We the Kids: The Preamble to the Constitution of the United States* (New York: Penguin Putnam, Dial, 2002)
With the actual words of the Preamble as the only text, cartoon-like illustrations follow a group of bumbling, diverse friends and their dog on a camping trip demonstrating the rights and responsibilities the Constitution describes.
QUESTION FOR EXPLORATION: What are the rights and responsibilities of people in a group, and of those in authority?

❼ PRODUCTION, DISTRIBUTION, AND CONSUMPTION

Karen Barbour, *Little Nino's Pizzeria* (San Diego: Harcourt Brace, Voyager Books, c1987)
Nino's father owns a pizzeria, sells it, then misses making pizzas for customers so much that he opens a new one.
QUESTION FOR EXPLORATION: How do people decide what to produce and what services to provide?

⑧ SCIENCE, TECHNOLOGY, AND SOCIETY

Meilo So, *The Emperor and the Nightingale* (New York: Simon and Schuster, 1992)

This story is a retelling of the classic Hans Christian Andersen tale of a Chinese emperor who replaced the singing of a real nightingale with a mechanical one, only to miss the friendship and uniqueness of the real nightingale.

QUESTION FOR EXPLORATION: How can science and technology be used to address individual, social, and global problems or issues?

⑨ GLOBAL CONNECTIONS

Sherry Garland, *The Lotus Seed* (San Diego: Harcourt Brace, Voyager Books, 1997)

Grandmother from Vietnam accidentally sees the last emperor cry and takes a lotus seed in remembrance of that day and her ruler. She keeps the lotus seed with her as she emigrates to America, struggles with her new life, and then watches as the seed is planted and grows into a beautiful flower for her and her family to enjoy and remember her past life.

QUESTION FOR EXPLORATION: How are people, places, and environments connected around the globe?

⑩ CIVIC IDEALS AND PRACTICES

Doreen Cronin, *Duck for President* (New York: Simon & Schuster, Atheneum, 2008)

Farmer Brown's animals use the power of the vote to elect Duck as head of the farm. Duck moves from the farm to the White House, humorously showing the power of the vote and nature of elections as he goes.

QUESTION FOR EXPLORATION: What are key democratic ideals and practices? 📰

NOTES

1. National Council for the Social Studies (NCSS), *National Curriculum Standards for Social Studies: A Framework for Teaching, Learning, and Assessment* (Silver Spring, MD: NCSS, 2010), 26.

2. *Ibid*, 17.

3. *Ibid*, 28.

The books cited in this chapter are recommended for their value in implementing the National Curriculum Standards for Social Studies and the Common Core State Standards in Grade 1. They can also be used to help to meet the following standards of the national Standards for the English Language Arts published in 1996 by the International Reading Association and National Council of Teachers of English.

2 Students read a wide range of literature from many periods in many genres to build an understanding of many dimensions (e.g., philosophical, ethical, aesthetic) of human experience.

3 Students apply a wide range of strategies to comprehend, interpret, evaluate, and appreciate texts. They draw on their prior experience, their interactions with other readers and writers, their knowledge of word meaning and of other texts, their word identification strategies, and their understanding of textual features (e.g., sound-letter correspondence, sentence structure, context, graphics)

International Reading Association (IRA) and National Council of Teachers of English (NCTE), *Standards for the English Language Arts* (Newark, DE and Urbana, IL: IRA and NCTE, 1996): 21, 22.

8 Second Grade

Barbara Knighton

The Little House
Written and illustrated by Virginia Lee Burton
Boston: Houghton Mifflin, 1942

This simple story about a house in the country has been read and enjoyed by generations of families. Virginia Lee Burton won a Caldecott Medal in 1943 for her beautiful portrayal of the changes a little house in the country faces as the city moves closer and closer. This book was also named as number 9 on the National Education Association Teacher's Top 100 Books for Children.[1]

The story begins as the owner builds the house on a picturesque hill in the country. He then declares, "This Little House shall never be sold for gold or silver" and that it will be there for the great-great grandchildren's great-great grandchildren to live in. The house then watches the seasons pass by and begins to wonder about the lights of the city in the distance. The amazingly detailed illustrations dominate the pages and give the teacher multiple opportunities to solicit answers from students about the changes as they occur.

Eventually, big changes do come about, beginning with a road built in front of the house. Next come gas stations, roadside stands and other small houses. More roads, more houses and bigger buildings are constructed, and the teacher helps learners transition from a yearlong timeline to one covering multiple years. Creating timelines is a way for students in

Social Studies Standards Themes
❷ TIME, CONTINUITY, AND CHANGE
❸ PEOPLE, PLACES, AND ENVIRONMENTS
❼ PRODUCTION, DISTRIBUTION, AND CONSUMPTION

Common Core Standards
READING: LITERATURE—GRADE 2
Key Ideas and Details
1. Ask and answer questions such as *who, what, where, when, why*, and *how* to demonstrate understanding of key details in a text.
3. Describe how characters in a story respond to major events and challenges.

Craft and Structure
5. Describe the overall structure of a story, including describing how the beginning introduces the story and the ending concludes the action.

Integration of Knowledge and Ideas
7. Use information gained from the illustrations and words in a print or digital text to demonstrate understanding of its characters, setting, or plot.

LANGUAGE STANDARDS—GRADE 2
Vocabulary Acquisition and Use
4. Determine or clarify the meaning of unknown and multiple-meaning words and phrases based on *grade 2 reading and content, …*

the early grades to demonstrate their understanding of Theme 2 of the national social studies standards, **TIME, CONTINUITY, AND CHANGE**. This theme suggests that "through the study of the past and its legacy, learners examine the institutions, values, and beliefs of people in the past, acquire skills in historical inquiry and interpretation, and gain an understanding of how important historical events and developments have shaped the modern world."[2] A suggested product for this theme is the construction of a timeline that indicates an understanding of a sequence of events.

Using the text and pictures, the teacher records a timeline with the students to summarize the changes taking place around the house. For each page, the class verbally adds one more event to the growing timeline. "First the house is built; then the seasons pass; next the road is built in front of the house. What happens now?" By orally rehearsing the timeline, the teacher is preparing the students to create the timeline themselves at the end of the story.

Learners in the early grades understand that there are many objects considered to be part of "the past." When asked, they can often name wagons, horses, outhouses, etc. as belonging to long ago. What they often misunderstand is that objects that are part of "the past" changed over time, and often didn't co-exist.

The pictures on the inside front and back covers of Burton's book show some changes in transportation over time. This provides an additional opportunity to create a timeline specific to transportation. Doing so allows students to "identify" examples of both continuity and change, as depicted in stories, photographs, and documents,"[3] a process that is part of the NCSS National Curriculum Standards Theme 2.

Some other standards-based concepts have natural connections to this book as well. According to Theme 3 of the national social studies standards, **PEOPLE, PLACES, AND ENVIRONMENTS**, learners should understand "…physical and human characteristics of the community…and the interactions of people in these places with the environment."[4] Learners should also understand the "factors influencing various community… patterns of human settlement…."[5] Both of these concepts are included in the following activities. Moreover, the changes that take place around the house, as economic development results in urban sprawl, offer an opportunity to introduce students to one of the objectives of Standards Theme 7, **PRODUCTION, DISTRIBUTION, AND CONSUMPTION**: "Learners will understand… what people and communities gain and give up when they make a decision."[6]

Class Activity 1
Creating Timelines

NCSS Curriculum Standard
❷ TIME, CONTINUITY, AND CHANGE

❸ PEOPLE, PLACES, AND ENVIRONMENTS

QUESTION FOR EXPLORATION EARLY GRADES
▶ How was life in the past similar to and different from life today?

PROCESSES EARLY GRADES
Learners will be able to...
▶ Identify examples of both continuity and change, as demonstrated in stories, photographs, and documents

PRODUCTS EARLY GRADES
Learners demonstrate understanding by...
▶ Constructing timelines that indicate an understanding of a sequence of events.

QUESTION FOR EXPLORATION EARLY GRADES
▶ How do people change the environment, and how does the environment influence human activity?

KNOWLEDGE EARLY GRADES
Learners will understand....
▶ Physical and human characteristics of the... community..., and the interactions of people in [the community] with the environment.

National Curriculum Standards for Social Studies, pp. 30, 32, 33, 34, 35.

Lesson Sequence

(over the course of 2 days)

▶ Obtain the earliest photograph of your community that you can find. Contact a local, county or state museum for assistance with this task. For comparison purposes, have at least one modern picture as well. Title companies often can help you obtain aerial views of the plats in your community.

▶ Display the photographs. *Discussion question: How are these photos alike in what they show? How are they different? What changes have occurred over time?*

▶ After students have had time to create a mental list of ideas (putting one finger in the air to signal each idea) have them Pair/Share by talking with a neighbor to create a list of similarities and differences in the landscape over time.

▶ As a class, record the changes in a chart similar to the one that follows:

Changes and Similarities

WHAT YOU SEE IN THE PAST	WHAT YOU SEE IN MODERN TIMES (TODAY)	ARE THESE THE SAME OR DIFFERENT?
horses for transportation	cars	different
trees	trees	same
people live together (communities)	communities	same
smaller buildings	high-rise office buildings	different

▶ Explain that you will be sharing a book that begins in the past and that students should watch and listen closely for changes that occur in the place where "The Little House" was built.

▶ Read through the first page of the book, emphasizing the phrase, "This Little House shall never be sold for gold or silver and she will live to see our great-great-grandchildren's great-great-grandchildren living in her."

- Continue reading the next several pages, having students point out the changes taking place in each picture on each page. This is the section that describes the seasons. You might want to revisit this later to create a separate chart showing the four seasons and their changes.
- Use this section of the story to create your first timeline together. This timeline will simply have four parts: spring, summer, fall, winter. These seasons should be familiar to students and will allow you easily to create a timeline focusing on the mechanics of drawing the line and adding information without having to juggle content at the same time. The mechanics include arrows at the beginning and end to indicate that time came before and will come after, as well as a way of dividing the line into appropriate segments. For example:

◄——— *Spring* ———*Summer* ———*Fall* ——— *Winter* ——►

- On the winter page, the timeline shifts from *a year* to *year after year*. Point out to the children that their timeline will need to grow as well. Underneath the current season timeline, draw another longer line (Figure 1).
- Place the arrow and starting point at the beginning of this new larger timeline. Discuss with the class what to call this spot using the guidelines of needing enough words to share the important

event, but with as few words as possible, e.g., "Built Little House." The second spot could be "Seasons pass."
- From here on out, you will point to the timeline and talk about what you might add, but don't interrupt the flow of the story by writing on the timeline as you go. Instead, verbally rehearse what you could record.
- Continue reading the book, discussing events that could be added to the timeline.
- After the story is finished, use the text as a resource to review the events for the timeline. You will use those you rehearsed, along with the book, to double check and make sure your timeline ideas are complete.
- Break the class into groups. If you have access to multiple copies of the book, provide each group with a copy. Give each group a piece of legal-size paper with the solid black timeline base already drawn.
- Each group will now create a timeline of the story. Have them start by copying the first four events from your timeline on the board. If time permits, allow them to draw quick sketches to match the words. You may want to determine how many events each group should include from those identified.
- At the end, the timelines can be posted together so that students can assess the accuracy of their own timeline in comparison to others.

Figure 1
Extended Timeline

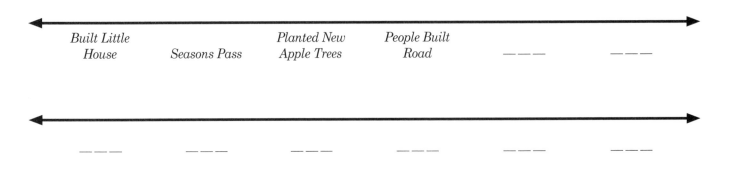

Class Activity 2
Changes in the Community

NCSS Curriculum Standard

❷ TIME, CONTINUITY, AND CHANGE

QUESTION FOR EXPLORATION EARLY GRADES
▶ How was life in the past similar to and different from life today?

PROCESSES EARLY GRADES
Learners will be able to...
▶ Identify examples of both continuity and change, as demonstrated in stories, photographs, and documents

❸ PEOPLE, PLACES, AND ENVIRONMENTS

QUESTION FOR EXPLORATION EARLY GRADES
▶ How do people change the environment, and how does the environment influence human activity?

KNOWLEDGE EARLY GRADES
Learners will understand...
▶ Factors influencing various community...patterns of human settlement

❼ PRODUCTION, DISTRIBUTION, AND CONSUMPTION

KNOWLEDGE EARLY GRADES
Learners will understand....
▶ What people and communities gain and give up when they make a decision.

National Curriculum Standards for Social Studies, pp. 30, 32, 34, 35, 51.

Lesson sequence

1. Begin today's lesson by showing the pictures of your community again. Review the chart you created about changes:

WHAT YOU SEE IN THE PAST	WHAT YOU SEE IN MODERN TIMES (TODAY)	ARE THESE THE SAME OR DIFFERENT?
horses for transportation	cars	different
trees	trees	same
people live together (communities)	communities	same
smaller buildings	high-rise office buildings	different

2. Then show the pictures from the book on page 1 and page 33, when the Little House is surrounded by the city.

3. Using both the timeline and the pictures, create a new chart detailing the causes and effects of changes described in the book. (See the information in chapter 3 of this volume related to introducing and practicing this skill.) These samples from the book should provide a way to start:

CAUSE	EVENT	RESULT FOR LITTLE HOUSE
Building a road	Gas stations, roadside stands, and houses	More roads, more houses, schools, etc
Need for transportation	Elevated train above the little house	Little house did not know the change in seasons
Replacing apartments and tenements	Building 25-35 story buildings	Little House became shabby and lonely

4. In a Pair/Share activity, have students discuss the impacts of the changes on the Little House. Which change for the house also had the greatest impact on people living nearby? Which change had the greatest impact on the land itself? Lead them to the conclusion that, although most changes seem to "hurt" the house, some changes seem beneficial and some seem hurtful to the people and land. This book does seem to be critical of urban sprawl and progress; therefore, it is important for the teacher to discuss both the benefits and drawbacks of changes to the environment.

5. In a follow up activity, either the same day or the next, lead a conversation about what people and communities gain and give up when they make economic decisions of the kind that affected the Little House. For example, people give up open space as there are more buildings, but gain more choices for shopping.

Reading Activities

These activities can help to meet the following Reading Standards for Literature and Language Standard from the Common Core State Standards for English Language Arts (Grade 2):

READING: LITERATURE—GRADE 2
Key Ideas and Details
1. Ask and answer questions such as *who, what, where, when, why,* and *how* to demonstrate understanding of key details in a text.
3. Describe how characters in a story respond to major events and challenges

Craft and Structure
5. Describe the overall structure of a story, including describing how the beginning introduces the story and the ending concludes the action.

Integration of Knowledge and Ideas
7. Use information gained from the illustrations and words in a print or digital text to demonstrate understanding of its characters, setting, or plot.

LANGUAGE—GRADE 2
Vocabulary Acquisition and Use
4. Determine or clarify the meaning of unknown and multiple-meaning words and phrases based on *grade 2 reading and content,* …

Common Core State Standards for English Language Arts and Literacy in History/Social Studies, Science, and Technical Subjects, p. 11 (Reading Literature); p. 27 (Language)

1. Asking and Answering Questions about Key Details

▸ On the first page, the builder predicts, *This Little House will never be sold for gold or silver and she will live to see our great-great-grandchildren's great-great-grandchildren living in her.* Was he correct? Do we find out in the book, or does this prediction remain a mystery?

▸ On pages 7 and 9, you begin to see a bit of a speck in the distance of the picture. *What do you suppose the author drew there in the picture? What could it be? Why is the land changing?*

▸ On page 18, it says that no one wants to live in the house or take care of her. *What could happen to the Little House as a result?*

▸ On page 35, they move the Little House. *Where might they move the Little House?*

2. Characterization

▸ In this text, the main character is unusual because it is the house itself. Talk about the difficulty in understanding the feelings and responses of a character that doesn't talk. Show students how the illustrations are used to add to the story, and how they help to convey how the house feels. Other characters in the story include the ancestors of the original owners/builders of the house. Discuss how there might have been things happening that don't show up in the book. For example, family members might have been talking about the house, sharing stories or even pictures. Those stories then lead to the family's decision to move the house in the end.

3. The Structure of the Story

▶ This story lends itself well to creating a "story mountain" or plot line. On your whiteboard or document reader, create a plot line showing the beginning, rising action, climax, and conclusion. Then, using the book, have students help you fill in the events showing how the changes around the house reflect rising action until the climax of the story where the house is moved back out to the country. Discuss whether this story could continue after the book ends, possibly becoming a circle story in which the same process of urban development around the house happens again.

4. Vocabulary Acquisition and Use

▶ Have children use the text and illustrations to create definitions of these words:

distance	curious
brook	harvest
surveyors	automobiles
tenement	trolley
elevated train	cellars
subway	shabby

▶ Have students create sentences about the story, using the words. Some examples are:
The Little House could see the city lights in the **distance.**
She was **curious** *about life in the city.*
The children were swimming in the **brook** *by the Little House.*
In the fall, the Little House could see the farmers **harvest** *the crops.*

5. Ellipses

▶ Throughout the text, the author uses ellipses many times to create a more dramatic reading. Begin on page 2 ("from the one before…"), pointing out the ellipses (e.g., on p. 12 , "year followed year…"). In this book, ellipses serve two purposes. The first is to emphasize the passage of time. The second use is to suggest multiple examples (p. 16, "Gasoline stations…roadside stands…").

▶ Reread the story, asking the children to point out the places where ellipses occur. As you find the examples, examine which purpose they have and use that to influence your voice and inflection as you read.

Text-to-text Comparison

▶ A similar book is *The House on Maple Street*, by Bonnie Pryor (New York: HarperCollins, 1992). It begins in the present and takes the reader back in time to when there was a stream and a forest in the place the family currently lives.

▶ After reading the book, create a timeline for the changes to the land where the family's house is located.

▶ Using the timeline from *The Little House* and this book, compare and contrast the two stories.

Other Recommended Books for the Second Grade Classroom

These books can be used to teach the nine social studies themes other than Theme 2, **TIME, CONTINUITY, AND CHANGE** (which is the principal theme featured in the above Activities). All books can be used to meet Standard 1 of the Common Core State Standards for Reading Literature for Grade 2: "Ask and answer such questions as *who, what, where, when, why*, and *how* to demonstrate understanding of key details in a text." As teachers review the books, they can use the chart of standards on pp. 8–9 to develop strategies for meeting other Common Core Standards for Reading Literature in Grade 2 when they use the books in class.

❶ CULTURE

Norah Dooley, *Everybody Bakes Bread* (Minneapolis, MN: Lerner, Carolrhoda Books, 1996)
Carrie is sent out into her neighborhood on a fool's errand for her mother after arguing with her brother. As she stops at each neighbor's house, each family greets Carrie while baking a different type of bread. This book and its multiethnic neighborhood provide several different examples of this every day staple.
QUESTION FOR EXPLORATION: How are groups of people alike and different?

❸ PEOPLE, PLACES, AND ENVIRONMENTS

Mari Takabayashi, *I Live in Brooklyn* (New York: Houghton Mifflin, 2004)
Michelle and her family live in Brooklyn. In this book, she tells about her day, including all the places she visits in New York City. This book provides an opportunity to compare an urban lifestyle to suburban or rural life.
QUESTION FOR EXPLORATION: What are similarities and differences between places near and far?

❹ INDIVIDUAL DEVELOPMENT AND IDENTITY

Maya Aimera and John D. Ivanko, *To Be a Kid* (Watertown, MA: Charlesbridge Publishing, 1991)
Several countries are represented in this colorful book, which is filled with photographs of children at play. It is a book with few words, allowing the teacher to guide children, through discussion, to an understanding that although the specifics may change, there are many similarities in childhood experiences throughout the world.
QUESTION FOR EXPLORATION: How am I different from and similar to others?

❺ INDIVIDUALS, GROUPS, AND INSTITUTIONS

Dyanne DiSalvo-Ryan, *Uncle Willie and the Soup Kitchen* (New York: HarperCollins, 1997)
Uncle Willie brings his nephew to the soup kitchen where he works to let him find out how satisfying it can be to help others. This book, which was a Notable Social Studies Trade Book in 1992, provides a nonthreatening way to introduce the ideas of people in our communities needing our help and how we can work together for the common good.
QUESTION FOR EXPLORATION: How do civic, governmental, and religious organizations function in our community, state, and nation?

❻ POWER, AUTHORITY, AND GOVERNANCE

Joan Blos, *Old Henry* (New York: HarperCollins, 1990)
Old Henry moves into a run-down shack and starts to feel right at home. However, his neighbors start to fuss about the need to fix it up. Henry, feeling pressured, moves out. Eventually, the mayor gets involved to work out a compromise. Teachers can use this book as a basis for asking children to develop possible solutions to a community problem.
QUESTION FOR EXPLORATION: What are the rights and responsibilities of citizens in a constitutional democracy?

❼ PRODUCTION, DISTRIBUTION, AND CONSUMPTION

Donald Hall, *Ox-Cart Man* (New York: Puffin, 1983)
This tale, the 1990 Caldecott Medal winner, is set in the 19th century and begins with a rural family packing up an ox-cart with the many hand-made products they are preparing to sell. The father takes the cart to town and sells the items, including the cart and his beloved ox. Then he goes about purchasing the items that the family needs but can't produce on their own. This is a great way to introduce the idea of producers and consumers.

QUESTION FOR EXPLORATION: How do people decide what goods and services to produce and consume?

❽ SCIENCE, TECHNOLOGY, AND SOCIETY

Jacqueline Briggs Martin, *Snowflake Bentley* (New York: Houghton Mifflin, 1998)
This biography of photographer and inventor Wilson Bentley shows how a man turned a childhood fascination about snowflakes into a scientific career. The story will enthrall students as they listen to the trials and failures "Snowflake Bentley" encountered along the way to success. This true and inspiring story won the 1999 Caldecott medal.

QUESTION FOR EXPLORATION: What are examples of science and technology that have impacted individuals and society?

❾ GLOBAL CONNECTIONS

Beatrice Hollyer, *Wake Up World: A Day in the Life of Children Around the World* (New York: Henry Holt, 1999)
This book follows the lives of eight children from eight different countries. Each two-page spread covers a different aspect of common daily life and is full of photographs. Students can begin to explore the wants and needs of people around the world and how they meet those needs.

QUESTION FOR EXPLORATION: What are the effects of increasing global connections?

❿ CIVIC IDEALS AND PRACTICES

Willie Perdomo, *Clemente!* (New York: Henry Holt, 2011)
Roberto Clemente is the first Latin American inducted into the Baseball Hall of Fame. This 2011 Notable Social Studies Trade Book not only talks about his life, but touches on his charity work throughout Latin America. It's always a great idea to find a book that brings students' interests and hobbies into the classroom. Clemente's name is one that many students might already know, and seeing a familiar, famous person who believes in giving back can encourage students to adopt similar ideals.

QUESTION FOR EXPLORATION: How can we apply civic ideals and practices in home, school, and the community? 📘

The books cited in this chapter are recommended for their value in implementing the National Curriculum Standards for Social Studies and the Common Core State Standards for English Language Arts in Grade 2. They can also be used to help to meet the following standards from the national Standards for the English Language Arts published in 1996 by the International Reading Association and National Council of Teachers of English.

2 Students read a wide range of literature from many periods in many genres to build an understanding of many dimensions (e.g., philosophical, ethical, aesthetic) of human experience.

3 Students apply a wide range of strategies to comprehend, interpret, evaluate, and appreciate texts. They draw on their prior experience, their interactions with other readers and writers, their knowledge of word meaning and of other texts, their word identification strategies, and their understanding of textual features (e.g., sound-letter correspondence, sentence structure, context, graphics)

International Reading Association (IRA) and National Council of Teachers of English (NCTE), *Standards for the English Language Arts* (Newark, DE and Urbana, IL: IRA and NCTE, 1996): 21, 22.

NOTES

1. The NEA Teacher's Top 100 list was compiled from an online survey in 2007. See http://www.nea.org/grants/13154.htm

2. National Council for the Social Studies (NCSS), *National Curriculum Standards for Social Studies: A Framework for Teaching, Learning, and Assessment* (Silver Spring, MD: NCSS, 2010), 30.

3. *Ibid.*, 32.

4. *Ibid.*, 35.

5. *Ibid.*

6. *Ibid.*, 51.

Third Grade

Linda Bennett and Leanna Guillory

Show Way
**Written by Jacqueline Woodson,
illustrated by Hudson Talbott**

New York: Penguin, G.P. Putnam's Sons, 2005

This 2006 Newbery Honor Book uses a red thread, two needles, and a piece of muslin to depict the family history of the author, Jacqueline Woodson. The vivid multimedia illustrations by Hudson Talbott include watercolor and chalk collages that add rich images and depth to the struggles and joys of the women in the author's family. There is also a montage page of historic photographs and newspaper articles from the civil rights movement of the 1960's, and another of quotations from African American authors and leaders.

Show Way is the story of how the women within one family artistically quilted the directions for a path to freedom or showed the way for others and the next generation. Throughout the book, the quilt making traditions are passed down from generation to generation as the women share their lives together while growing up as African American women. Women from slavery, the civil rights movement and the present are included in the quilt patterns, which reveal trails of the eight generations of women. The author wrote the book to share her family history with her daughter, Toshi Georgiana, to provide her with a "Show Way" or pathway of her ancestors' search for freedom.

The story begins when Soonie's great-grandmother is sold as a slave in Virginia, separated from her

Social Studies Standards Themes
⑩ CIVIC IDEALS AND PRACTICES
⑥ POWER, AUTHORITY, AND GOVERNANCE
❸ PEOPLE, PLACES, AND ENVIRONMENTS
❷ TIME, CONTINUITY, AND CHANGE

Common Core Standards
READING: LITERATURE—GRADE 3
Key Ideas and Details
1. Ask and answer questions to demonstrate understanding of a text, referring explicitly to the text as the basis for the answers.
2. Recount stories, including fables, folktales, and myths from diverse cultures; determine the central message, lesson, or moral and explain how it is conveyed through key details in the text.
3. Describe characters in a story (e.g., their traits, motivations, or feelings) and explain how their actions contribute to the sequence of events.

Craft and Structure
4. Determine the meaning of words and phrases as they are used in a text, distinguishing literal from nonliteral language.

WRITING—GRADE 3
Text Types and Purposes
2. Write informative/exploratory texts to examine a topic and convey ideas and information clearly.

parents, and moved to a plantation in South Carolina. The great-grandmother was raised with other slave children and at night, listened to stories of growing up and becoming free. The next two generations of women, Soonie's grandmother and mother, were slaves in South Carolina as well.

As a young woman, Soonie learns to sew symbols such as the moon, stars, or roads into the design of the quilt to provide maps of secret routes to escape from slavery. She shares her quilt stories with others as they strive to be free. More than a century later during the 1960s, Soonie's great granddaughters, Caroline and Ann, march for civil rights. The story ends at the author's home in Brooklyn where she expresses joy and hope for her daughter as she discovers her Show Way or road in life.

Third grade students and teachers learn from the history of the women and from the metaphor of life's journey in the illustrations. The story leads the reader to learn about family heritage and wisdom from generations past. The symbolism within the quilt intrigues young children and motivates them to learn methods for using symbols and designs to tell a story. Story quilts serve as symbols for civic ideals and articulate the journey toward freedom and human rights. The actions of the women in the story demonstrate how the women took on a civic issue and participated in making a difference in the lives of others searching for freedom.

The first activity is based on social studies Theme 10, **CIVIC IDEALS AND PRACTICES**, with a focus on "How can we become informed and engage in meaningful civic action?" *Freedom for Shelter, Food and Clothing* is the title for the lesson, and students begin to understand the services that are available in their community to help people in need. As the lesson progresses, students have opportunities to engage in civic action.

To address NCSS Theme 3, **PEOPLE, PLACES, AND ENVIRONMENTS** for the Early Grades, the second lesson links to the question "How do simple geographic skills and tools help humans understand spatial relationships?" The way the women in the book used the moon, stars, and roads in the quilt to follow the route to freedom and the way students use a compass rose and legend today for helping people find locations are the focus of the lesson.

The richness of the text in *Show Way* provides a wealth of literacy skills as options for linking social studies and reading. Prior to reading the book, the students will activate schemes during a pre-reading graphic organizer activity to encourage them to share what they know about new concepts and complete the statement: "I know this because..." Understanding words such as "plantation," "slavery," or "tradition" can provide a strong base for understanding the context of the story. Activities for vocabulary development are included because there are terms in the book that are unique to the time and repeated phrases with which students need help in order to draw inferences. The book is rich with terminology and the historical context of the time so teachers need to assist students in understanding the meaning of the words. It may be valuable to read the book aloud and assist readers with text and inferences. By sharing stories from their families, the students can connect the book to the world, themselves, and their writing. As students write about their families and put the pieces of their stories together, they will learn to develop a story using specific details. The teacher can find ways to scaffold learning by intertwining the knowledge and skills in literacy and social studies to build a unit to meet third grade curriculum standards and instructional goals.

Nine third grade books for the remainder of the Ten Themes of Social Studies and brief annotations are provided at the end of the chapter. The book itself could easily be used in lessons on the NCSS Themes of ❶ **CULTURE**, ❷ **TIME, CONTINUITY AND CHANGE**, or ❹ **INDIVIDUAL DEVELOPMENT AND IDENTITY**. In addition, Jacqueline Woodson's book, *The Other Side* (New York: Penguin Putnam, 2001) or *The Keeping Quilt* by Patricia Polacco (New York: Simon and Schuster, 2010) could be incorporated into the current activities.

Freedom for Shelter, Food, and Clothing

NCSS Curriculum Standard

⑩ CIVIC IDEALS AND PRACTICES

QUESTIONS FOR EXPLORATION EARLY GRADES

▶ How can we apply civic ideals and practices in home, school, and the community?

▶ How can we become informed and engage in meaningful civic action?

KNOWLEDGE EARLY GRADES

Learners will understand...

▶ Concepts and ideals such as: individual dignity, fairness, freedom, the common good, rule of law, civic life, rights, and responsibilities

PRODUCTS EARLY GRADES

Learners demonstrate understanding by...

▶ Participating in civic discussion and action about a school or community issue;

▶ Drawing illustrations of examples of participation supportive of civic ideals and practices.

⑥ POWER, AUTHORITY, AND GOVERNANCE

PROCESSES EARLY GRADES

Learners will be able to...

▶ Examine issues involving the rights and responsibilities of individuals and groups in relation to the broader society.

National Curriculum Standards for Social Studies, pp. 62, 63, 65 (Civic Ideals and Practices); p. 48 (Power, Authority, and Governance).

Procedures

1. BIG QUESTION: *What freedoms do you have?* Introduce students to the Four Freedoms described by Franklin D. Roosevelt in his Address to Congress of January 6, 1941.

The Four Freedoms

1. Freedom of speech and expression.
2. Freedom of worship.
3. Freedom from want.
4. Freedom from fear.

From Franklin D. Roosevelt's Address to Congress, January 6, 1941.

2. BOOK REVIEW: From slavery and civil rights to today, the women in the book *Show Way* exemplify how to care for the well being of others. In the text and illustrations, the muslin fabric and the needle depict the support offered by different generations of women for each other. The quilt images in the book illustrate how the women used their talents to sew quilt squares for people to find safe places to stay and a route to a new life. The fabric of peoples' lives is intertwined through the use of muslin and thread to make clothing and a quilt for a place to rest.

The women in the *Show Way* tell their daughters and granddaughter that "there is a road to growing up tall and straight boned" and "loved those babies up." The women are models for encouraging children to be strong and feel the love of family. There is a woman nurturing each girl and teaching her how the quilt is a symbol of strength and represents their bond as a family. For example, Grandma Soonie sewed a patch of the Show Way in Ann's and Caroline's dresses during the Civil Rights era, and they touched it when they became scared or frightened by civil unrest. As the reader observes the appearance and interactions of the women in the book, the joy of being in a family, and the support of each generation to teach the next one how to hold onto the tradition of sewing is apparent.

3. ENGAGE: Show and discuss images of places in your community that provide shelter, food or clothing.

4. BEGINNING: Using electronic or print resources, search the yellow pages, community listings, or newspapers for food banks, soup kitchens, second hand clothing, temporary housing, shelters, or other services. Record the names and locations of service providers or groups to help people in your community with food, clothing, and shelter. Alternate: Invite as a guest speaker someone who lives in a home built by Habitat for Humanity or has worked at or eaten at a Soup Kitchen.

5. EXPLORE: Mark on a map where the services are located in your community. Search for groups that could provide services for your community if there were an emergency. Alternate: Make a community flyer that shows the locations and describes the services offered in the community.

6. EXPLAIN: How do these services help the community?

What can you do to help provide others with food, clothing or shelter in our community?
What group in our school can help? (After-school clubs, PTA, classrooms)
What can you do to show others how to help?

7. ELABORATE: Develop and implement a plan for the students to distribute their map or flyer in the school or community.

8. EVALUATION: A map or flyer on community services will be assessed for accurate information and usability.
Students' reflections on the following questions will be discussed or collected.

People in my community are being responsible to the needs of others by _____.

The places in my community where there is free or inexpensive food, clothing and shelter are _____, _____, or _____.

One way that I can be a good citizen is _____ _____.

Extension: Students can combine this lesson with the next one, so that the map or flyer about freedoms includes a compass rose and legend.

Showing the Way

NCSS Curriculum Standards

❸ PEOPLE, PLACES, AND ENVIRONMENTS

QUESTION FOR EXPLORATION EARLY GRADES

▶ How do simple geographic skills and tools help humans understand spatial relationships?

KNOWLEDGE EARLY GRADES

Learners will understand...

▶ Cultural patterns and their interactions within and across places, such as migration and settlement, changes in customs and ideas, and in the ways people make a living;

▶ Tools such as maps, globes, and geospatial technologies in investigating the relationships among people, places, and environments.

PRODUCTS EARLY GRADES

Learners demonstrate understanding by...

▶ Constructing a map depicting the school, community, state, or region that demonstrates an understanding of relative location, direction, boundaries, and significant physical features.

❷ TIME, CONTINUITY, AND CHANGE

PRODUCTS EARLY GRADES

Learners demonstrate understanding by...

▶ Using artifacts in discussions and reports to offer explanations about life in the past.

National Curriculum Standards for Social Studies, pp. 34, 35, 37 (People, Places, and Environments); p. 33 (Time, Continuity, and Change).

Procedures

1. BIG QUESTION: How do you find your way to a location?

2. BEGINNING: As a class, look back through the book *Show Way* to investigate the words or images that were used to provide directions for the paths of the women, or describe freedom trails or other journeys in the book. As students share, list or sketch the ideas on the whiteboard or chart paper. Alternate idea: Listen to a song about routes to freedom ("Follow the Drinking Gourd").

3. MAKING CONNECTIONS: As a class, look at the elements of a map, such as the key or legend, grid lines, scales, colors or compass rose (Figure 1). These are tools that help us find our way to a location. How did the women use the stars, moon,

Figure 1

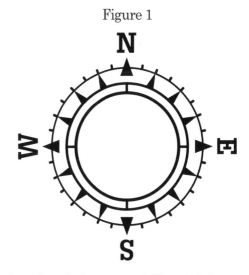

and road as their compass? How did the maps show the route to a location? Did the quilts contain directions to a place? How did the design of quilt squares describe a specific location? What shapes did the squares have to show directions?

Define the term "compass rose." Discuss with students how they might use the compass rose or other legends and how their use is different from or similar to the methods used by the women in the book to show others the way. If possible, add images of legends—past and present.

4. DEVELOP AND CARRY OUT A PLAN: In pairs, students work to make a map either of the school and its grounds, or of the neighborhood, that includes a compass rose and legend. Other students should be able to use the directions to find a route to a location.

Based on the developmental level of students and the focus of the lesson, a specific location may be selected for the product. The depiction could include a familiar place and at least two to four other landmarks, buildings or natural features near the familiar place to demonstrate an understanding of relative location. The depiction needs boundaries such as walls, perimeters, or fences. The physical features might be doors, computers, tables, buildings, or trees. Remember to discuss the maps with students because they will share information that may not be evident in the map.

One appropriate activity is a map of the school whose objective is to use the directions to tell someone how to get from the main office to their classroom. The school map might have rooms such as the cafeteria, classrooms, and media center, and the locations could be relative to the main office or their classroom. The school map could have the outside space or the walls of the building as the boundary. The physical features might be doors, windows, desks, or computers.

5. EVALUATION: The teacher listens to discussions by students using the terminology that has been taught and observes the verbal directions by students explaining how to use the legend and compass rose. The peer feedback on the visual representation of the compass rose and legend helps clarify the work of the students and their accuracy in completing the task.

EXTENSION: The students could make a map showing the directions for getting from one location, such as the school, to a community service that provides food, clothing or shelter.

Discuss how maps in the book and maps today provide a guide to finding our way.

Reading Activities

The teacher can guide reading and discussion of this book by the class to help to meet the following Grade 3 Reading Standards for Literature from the Common Core State Standards for English Language Arts.

Key Ideas and Details
1. Ask and answer questions to demonstrate understanding of a text, referring explicitly to the text as the basis for the answers.
2. Recount stories, including fables, folktales, and myths from diverse cultures; determine the central message, lesson, or moral and explain how it is conveyed through key details in the text.
3. Describe characters in a story (e.g., their traits, motivations, or feelings) and explain how their actions contribute to the sequence of events.

Craft and Structure
4. Determine the meaning of words and phrases as they are used in a text, distinguishing literal from nonliteral language.

Common Core State Standards for English Language Arts & Literacy in History/Social Studies, Science, and Technical Subjects, p. 12.

Activate Schema

Learners will understand that good readers activate prior knowledge to help them understand new information. They will use prior knowledge/schema to engage with the text before, during, and after reading.

Learners will demonstrate understanding by using a graphic organizer (The Frame) in cooperative groups to brainstorm the meaning of new vocabulary.

Procedures

▸ The teacher will divide the class into groups of four students.
▸ Each group will be given a piece of chart paper with two concentric circles drawn in the middle. Each group of students will be given one of the target words to put in the smaller circle. The target words to be given are: plantation, slavery, tradition, and quilt. The same target word can be given to multiple groups.
▸ In the area of the larger circle, the students will record what they know about the target word. The teacher should encourage them to consider who, what, when, where, and how during their brainstorming.
▸ The students will then draw a frame (large box) that includes sufficient space for writing (see Figure 2, p. 80). In that outside space they will respond to the prompt "I know this because…" Possible answers might be: I have learned about this in another class, I have read about this in a book, my family has discussed this before, I have seen a movie about this, etc.

▸ In a large group area or in front of the class each group will share what they know about their word. Groups who have the same word can present together. The teacher will guide the discussion so that accurate meanings of the words are established.

Alternate Lesson—Museum Tour

▸ The teacher will divide the class into groups of four students.
▸ Each group will be given a piece of chart paper with a circle drawn in the middle. Each group of students will be given the same target word to put in the center of the circle. The teacher will assign either the word *slavery* or the word *tradition* as the target word.
▸ In the space around the outside of the circle, the students will record what they know about the target word. The teacher should encourage them to consider who, what, when, where, and how during their brainstorming.

Figure 2
Graphic Organizer for Vocabulary

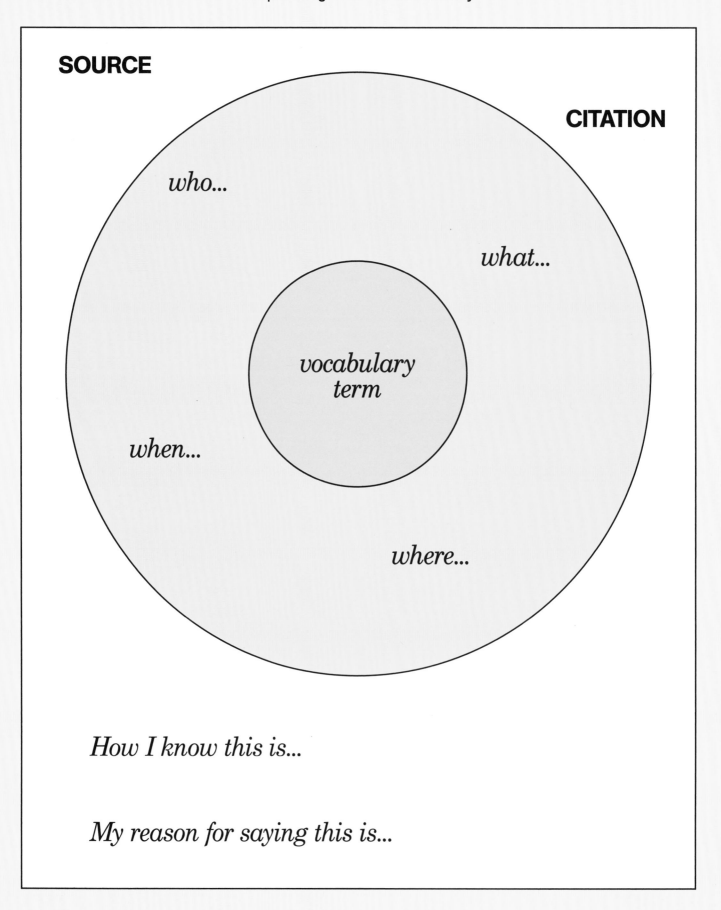

- The students will then draw a frame (large box) around the outside of their brainstorming. In that outside space they will answer the question "I know this because..." Possible answers might be: I have learned about this in another class, I have read about this in a book, my family has discussed this before, I have seen a movie about this, etc.
- The teacher will explain that in order to broaden their knowledge about the target word they will go on a "museum tour." Each group will decide on a recorder who will record new facts they learn as they visit other groups. They will also decide who will serve as the docent, a person who will stay with their chart and share information with visiting groups.
- As the students rotate around the room visiting each "display," the docent will share information from their chart about the target word. The recorder from the visiting group will write down new information they hear.
- Students will then go back to their group and add new information to their chart in the brainstorming area.
- In a large group area or in front of the whole group, each group will share 2-3 facts about the target word and how they know the information they are sharing.
- The teacher will guide the discussion so that accurate meanings of the words are established.

Inferences
- Learners will use prior knowledge, questioning, and connections to draw inferences.
- Learners will demonstrate understanding orally in a large group setting by making inferences about words and phrases in the text to deepen understanding when the book is read aloud.

Procedures
- Prepared in advance, the teacher will write the following phrases from the book on chart paper, leaving space for thinking under each phrase.

patch of land	girl-child
piece of quilt	she loved her up
jumped broom	Trail to the North
straight-boned	Show Way

- The students will gather in a large group area in front of the chart paper.
- The teacher will explain that the book is full of interesting words and phrases that are very different from how we speak today. In order to better understand the story, students will infer what they think the words and phrases mean.
- The teacher will lead a discussion about each word, recording every suggestion about each word on the chart paper. Students will share what background knowledge they have that helped them understand the words.
- The teacher will read the book, *Show Way*.
- The teacher will revisit the words and lead a discussion about what the students know about the meaning of the phrases after the book was read.

Revisiting Schema
- After the book is read, the teacher will lead a discussion about how the language in the book is different from the language spoken today. The teacher can refer back to the previous activities for words or phrases, or the students can make comparisons on their own. Other discussion points might be:
  Why do you think the language is different?
  Why do you think the language changed?

Making Connections
- Learners will identify and explain relevant connections between texts and other cultures, settings, people, and historic periods.
- The students will demonstrate understanding by recording "text-to-self" and "text-to-text" connections in their reading journal and by oral presentation.
  TEXT-TO-SELF: The teacher leads a discussion about family traditions. The students write a

text-to-self connection, keeping in mind the traditions of their own families. They illustrate their connection on a piece of white construction paper. In a large group area the students present their illustrations and share details about their text-to-self connection to the class.

TEXT-TO-TEXT: During a partnership reading situation, the teacher will provide the following books:

Grandaddy's Street Songs by Monalisa DeGross (New York: Hyperion, Jump at the Sun, 1999). This is a heartwarming book about a grandfather sharing the traditions of street vending, which was his profession in the long-ago days.

The Always Prayer Shawl by Sheldon Oberman (Honesdale, PA: Boyds Mills Press, 1993). This book is about a Jewish boy who leaves Czarist Russia with his family to come to America. He leaves behind a beloved grandfather who gives the boy his prayer shawl. Along with handing down the prayer shawl to several generations, the name Adam is also passed down. This book won a National Jewish Book Award and Sydney Taylor Book Award.

Betty Doll by Patricia Polacco (New York: Penguin Puffin, 2004). In a letter left to her daughter after her death, Mary Ellen explains how her handmade doll, Betty Doll, came to be and how the doll played a very important role in her life.

The Keeping Quilt by Patricia Polacco (New York: Simon and Schuster, 1988). Patricia Polacco shares her own story of the Keeping Quilt, which was passed from mother to daughter for centuries. This book won a National Jewish Book Award and Sydney Taylor Picture Book Award.

Writing Activity

This activity can help to meet the following Writing Standard from the Common Core State Standards for English Language Arts (Grade 3)

WRITING—GRADE 3
Text Types and Purposes
2. Write informative/exploratory texts to examine a topic and convey ideas and information clearly.

Common Core State Standards for English Language Arts and Literacy in History/Social Studies, Science and Technical Subjects, p.12.

Learners will write a story using details that are specific, relevant, and focused. Learners will reread and revise their story, taking account of their audience and the purpose, content, organization, sentence structure, and word choice of the story. Learners will also write for an extended amount of time during a writing workshop.

Learners will demonstrate understanding by producing a piece of quality writing following the procedures below.

Option 1: The students will interview a member of their family about a family tradition or family story.

Option 2: The students will bring an object to school that represents a family tradition or family story.

Either of these options can be shared in a group setting as a before- or after-writing activity.

Procedures
▶ The students will use a writing plan to organize their thoughts.
▶ The students will use one of the above options to write a story about their family tradition or family story.
▶ The students' story must include three topic paragraphs, a beginning, and an appropriate ending.
▶ The students will pair/share to determine if any changes need to be made in their stories.
▶ The students will make necessary changes using, as a guide the writing rubric on the next page, which was developed by Columbia Public Schools, Columbia, MO.

Rubric for Writing Activity

COMPONENT	NEEDS IMPROVEMENT 1	NEARING PROFICIENT 2	PROFICIENT 3	ADVANCED 4
Organization *Telling the story so that the reader is able to understand the message*	Lacks evidence of a beginning, middle and/or end	Provides evidence of a beginning, middle, and end	Writes a beginning, middle, and end	Writes an effective beginning that leads into a well-developed middle and an ending that ties the piece together
Focus and Coherence *Connecting ideas together around a central topic*	Provides unrelated ideas and is difficult to follow	Provides some evidence of a controlling idea but does not maintain a clear focus	Provides a controlling idea and maintains focus throughout most of the piece	Provides a clear controlling idea and maintains a clear focus throughout the piece
	Lacks transitions	Uses repetitive or few transitions	Uses transitional words and/or phrases	Uses effective transitional words and/or phrases throughout the piece
Development *Strategies the writer uses to develop the story and its message*	Attempts to address the topic but lacks development	Generally addresses the topic, but may provide some details that are not relevant	Addresses the topic and provides relevant details/examples	Clearly addresses the topic and provides specific and relevant details/examples
	Uses words that are consistently repetitive, dull, and colorless	Uses words that tend to be repetitive, imprecise, and ordinary	Uses some words that are specific, accurate, and related to the topic	Uses words that are specific, accurate, and suited to the topic
	Shows little or no awareness of audience and purpose	Shows some awareness of audience and purpose	Shows an awareness of audience and purpose	Clearly shows an awareness of audience and purpose
Mechanics *The use of grammar, punctuation, usage, and sentence structure*	Includes incomplete sentences that are distracting to the reader	Contains some incomplete sentences that may be distracting to the reader	Generally uses complete sentences	Consistently uses complete sentences
	Contains repeated errors in grammar/ usage, punctuation, capitalization and/ or spelling that may be distracting to the reader	Contains errors in grammar/ usage, punctuation, capitalization and/ or spelling that may be distracting to the reader	May contain some errors in grammar/ usage, punctuation, capitalization and/ or spelling that are not significantly distracting to the reader	Contains few errors in grammar/ usage, punctuation, capitalization, and/or spelling

Columbia Public Schools, Columbia, MO Language Arts Department, 3rd Grade Writing Scoring Guide (*Revised January 2010*).

Other Recommended Books for the Third Grade Classroom

The following books can be used to teach the nine social studies themes other than Theme 10, **CIVIC IDEALS AND PRACTICES** (which is the principal focus of Activity 1 above). All the books can be used to meet Standard 1 of the Common Core Reading Standards for Literature (Grade 3): "Ask and answer questions to demonstrate understanding of a text, referring explicitly to the text as the basis for the answers." As teachers review the books, they can use the chart of standards on pp. 8–9 to develop strategies for meeting other Common Core Standards for Reading Literature in Grade 3 when they use the books in class.

❶ CULTURE

Allen Say, *Grandfather's Journey* (New York: Houghton Mifflin, 1993).
This 1994 Caldecott Medal Book is the tale of Say's grandfather, who leaves his home in Japan to live in California. The family struggles as its members grow in appreciation for both places as home.
QUESTION FOR EXPLORATION: How are groups of people alike and different?

❷ TIME, CONTINUITY, AND CHANGE

Laura Ingalls Wilder, *Little House on the Prairie* (New York: HarperCollins, 1953)
In this book from the popular *Little House* series, Pa Ingalls sells the log house in Wisconsin and moves the family to Kansas where they build a house on the prairie.
QUESTION FOR EXPLORATION: How was life in the past similar to and different from life today?

❸ PEOPLE, PLACES, AND ENVIRONMENTS

Liz Garton Scanlon, *All the World* (New York: Simon and Schuster, Beach Lane Books, 2009)
The main character, his sister, and parents spend the day together sharing locations such as the farmer's market, lunch in a café, and night at home. This book won a Caldecott Honor in 2010.
QUESTION FOR EXPLORATION: How do simple geographic skills and tools help humans understand spatial relationships?

❹ INDIVIDUAL DEVELOPMENT AND IDENTITY

Kate DiCamillo, *Because of Winn-Dixie* (Somerville, MA: Candlewick Press, 2000)
In this 2001 Newbery Honor Book, ten-year-old Opal meets unusual residents in her new hometown in Florida with her dog, Winn-Dixie, as she finds her place in the world.
QUESTION FOR EXPLORATION: How have others influenced who I am and who I am becoming?

❺ INDIVIDUALS, GROUPS, AND INSTITUTIONS

Richard Atwater, *Mr. Popper's Penguins* (Boston: Little, Brown and Co., 1938)
Throughout the book, the reader is amused by the adventures of 12 penguins that join the Popper family. This classic story was a Newbery Honor Book in 1939.
QUESTION FOR EXPLORATION: How do the groups to which I belong influence me, and how do I influence them?

❻ POWER, AUTHORITY, AND GOVERNANCE

Ken Mochizuki, *Passage to Freedom: The Sugihara Story* (New York: Lee & Low Books, 1997)
This story about Chiune Sugihara tells how one Japanese diplomat's devotion to justice led him to issue visas to Polish Jews during World War II, resulting in the survival of thousands.
QUESTION FOR EXPLORATION: What are the rights and responsibilities of people in a group, and of those in authority?

➐ PRODUCTION, DISTRIBUTION, AND CONSUMPTION

Katie Smith Milway, *One Hen—How One Small Loan Made a Big Difference.* (Tonawanda, NY: Kids Can Press, 2008)

Based on a true story, Kojo, a little boy in Ghana, buys a hen with a few coins from his mother's microfinance loan, which creates the largest poultry farm in West Africa.

QUESTION FOR EXPLORATION: How do we make choices about scarce resources?

➑ SCIENCE, TECHNOLOGY, AND SOCIETY

Gene Baretta, *Neo Leo: The Ageless Ideas of Leonardo da Vinci* (New York: Henry Holt and Company, 2009)

Leonardo's notebooks show that he thought of ideas for helicopters, tanks, hang gliders, contact lenses, robots and more — centuries before they were actually built.

QUESTION FOR EXPLORATION: What are some examples of science and technology that have impacted individuals and society?

➒ GLOBAL CONNECTIONS

Beatrice Hollyer, in association with Oxfam. *Wake Up, World: A Day In The Life Of Children Around The World* (New York: Henry Holt, 1999)

Children from eight different countries share details of their daily lives and insights on their culture and location in the world.

QUESTION FOR EXPLORATION: How are people, places and environments connected around the globe?

The books cited in this chapter are recommended for their value in implementing the National Curriculum Standards for Social Studies and the Common Core State Standards for English Language Arts in Grade 3. They can also be used to help to meet the following standards of the national Standards for the English Language Arts published in 1996 by the International Reading Association and National Council of Teachers of English.

1 Students read a wide range of print and nonprint texts to build an understanding of texts, of themselves, and of the cultures of the United States and the world; to acquire new information; to respond to the needs and demands of society and the workplace; and for personal fulfillment. Among these texts are fiction and nonfiction, classic and contemporary works.

2 Students read a wide range of literature from many periods in many genres to build an understanding of many dimensions (e.g., philosophical, ethical, aesthetic) of human experience.

International Reading Association (IRA) and National Council of Teachers of English (NCTE), *Standards for the English Language Arts* (Newark, DE and Urbana, IL: IRA and NCTE, 1996): 19, 21.

10 Fourth Grade

Carol Carney Warren

The Unbreakable Code

Written by Sara Hoagland Hunter, illustrated by Julia Miner

Flagstaff, AZ: Rising Moon Books, 1996. Now published by Cooper Square Publishing, Lanham, MD, and distributed by NBN Books (www.nbnbooks.com), 1-800-462-6420.

This beautifully illustrated book, chosen as a 1996 Smithsonian Notable Book for Children, imparts the warm and touching story of how a grandfather shares an important part of his culture with his grandson.

Young John must leave his home on the Navajo Reservation and move with his mother and stepfather to Minnesota. He does not want to leave and hides so no one can find him. Grandfather does locate John, however, and assures him that all will be well because wherever he goes, John will always have an unbreakable code with him. What is this unbreakable code?

Social Studies Standards Themes
❶ CULTURE
❸ PEOPLE, PLACES, AND ENVIRONMENTS

Other Related Themes
❷ TIME, CONTINUITY, AND CHANGE
❽ SCIENCE, TECHNOLOGY, AND SOCIETY
❿ CIVIC IDEALS AND PRACTICES

Common Core Standards

READING: LITERATURE—GRADE 4
Key Ideas and Details
1. Refer to details and examples in a text when explaining what the text says explicitly and when drawing inferences from the text.
2. Determine a theme of a story, drama, or poem from details in the text; summarize the text.

READING: FOUNDATIONAL SKILLS—GRADE 4
Phonics and Word Recognition
3. Know and apply grade-level phonics and word analysis skills in decoding words.
   (a) Use combined knowledge of all letter-sound correspondences, syllabication patterns, and morphology (e.g., roots and affixes) to read accurately unfamiliar multisyllabic words in context and out of context.

LANGUAGE—GRADE 4
Conventions of Standard English
2. Demonstrate command of the conventions of standard English capitalization, punctuation, and spelling when writing.
   (b) Use commas and quotation marks to mark direct speech and quotations from a text.

Vocabulary Acquisition and Use
4. Determine or clarify the meaning of unknown and multiple-meaning words and phrases based on *grade 4 reading and content*, choosing flexibly from a range of strategies.
   (a) Use context (e.g., definitions, examples, or restatements in text) as a clue to the meaning of a word or phrase.

5. Demonstrate understanding of figurative language, word relationships, and nuances in word meanings.
   (a) Explain the meaning of simple similes and metaphors (e.g., "as pretty as a picture") in context.

Grandfather, speaking gently in Navajo, explains the unbreakable code to John.

The unbreakable code is the Navajo language, and grandfather explains how it saved his life in World War II. He tells John that he must never forget his language, wherever he may go. Grandfather knows it will be difficult for John, just as it was for him when, as a child, he was sent to a government boarding school. Although punished for speaking Navajo at the school, Grandfather never forgot his native language. When grandfather was a teenager, World War II broke out, and the Navajo language became an unbreakable code that would help the United States win that war.

Grandfather shares important elements of the Navajo culture with his grandson, which makes this book particularly suitable for teaching the concepts of Theme 1, **CULTURE**, in the NCSS *National Curriculum Standards for Social Studies*. The learning expectations attached to this theme include questions for exploration, knowledge concepts, processes, and products that young learners encounter in studying the role of culture in society and in their own lives. In the early grades, young learners want to know more about others. Learners begin to explore and describe the ways cultures address human needs and concerns as well as ways in which language, stories, folktales, music and artistic creations serve as expressions of culture.

As the teacher reads *The Unbreakable Code*, she or he has students point out ways in which John's life is similar to and different from theirs. John's grandfather explains how the Navajo language was important to him as a child and young man and that this language will also connect John to his people. The teacher can ask some of the questions derived from Theme 1, **CULTURE**: "What are the common characteristics of different cultures? What does language tell us about the culture?" Students in fourth grade

are aware that other people in their community or classroom may come from different cultures and speak other languages, just as John and Grandfather spoke both Navajo and English. Perhaps the students themselves are bilingual and, like John, share common characteristics with two cultures. Through prior reading, students may have learned about folktales, myths, art and other aspects of various cultures around the world and recognize how these elements are important to each culture.

Lessons related to other themes of the NCSS National Curriculum Standards can also be taught. Among these is Theme 2, **TIME, CONTINUITY, AND CHANGE**. The important role of the Navajo Code Talkers and the Navajo Code in World War II is introduced. Additional information about the code is given at the end of the book and students may wish to explore this subject further. Students could learn about other American Indian peoples who also used their language to help win the war (e.g., Hopi, Cherokee).

Another theme that this book can help to introduce is that of 8, **SCIENCE, TECHNOLOGY, AND SOCIETY**. The code was used in radio communications to transmit instant information that could be used by U.S. commanders. It could report important battlefield movements; for example, the code assigned words to request reinforcements, report machine gun fire, and describe approaching aircraft using the names of birds. (A dive bomber, for example, was described as a chickenhawk). Because the code was in a language unknown to the Japanese armed forces, the Japanese commanders could not understand it or take quick counteractions if they intercepted the communications.

Another theme of the *National Curriculum Standards for Social Studies* that is an important element of *The Unbreakable Code* is Theme 10, **CIVIC IDEALS AND PRACTICES**. Grandfather explains to John why he and the other Navajo Code Talkers decided to fight

The Unbreakable Code
by Sara Hoagland Hunter   Illustrated by Julia Miner

for the United States. Grandfather's explanation was that America was "Our Mother" and that we fight for what we love and what is ours. He and many others showed their civic responsibility and love of country as citizens of the United States during wartime.

One extended social studies activity for the book takes us back to the Culture theme. In this activity, students can learn about a traditional American Indian culture in their state or region of the country. As they explore the culture, they will begin to discover and then describe the ways in which it addresses the needs and concerns of the group as well as ways in which language, stories, folktales, music and artistic creations serve as expressions of the culture. Students will then compare one aspect of this culture with that of the Navajo to discover how culture connects to different physical environments.

The second extended activity takes us to Theme 3, **PEOPLE, PLACES, AND ENVIRONMENTS**. Students view more closely the beautiful, realistic illustrations of the book. In this way, they enter the plateau region of the Southwestern United States. As they learn about this landform, students distinguish its characteristics from that of other landforms of the United States, and reflect on ways in which people adapt to and interact with their environment.

The reading activities presented in this chapter also offer pre- and post-reading practice suggestions in the areas of Inference, Vocabulary, Phonics and Word Recognition, Commas and Quotation Marks, Figurative Language, and Practice with Frequently Confused Words. The chapter closes with nine Fourth Grade books, including brief annotations, that relate to the standards themes other than **CULTURE**.

Studying an American Indian Culture in Your State or Region

NCSS Curriculum Standard

❶ CULTURE

KNOWLEDGE EARLY GRADES

Learners will understand...

▶ "Culture" refers to the behaviors, beliefs, values, traditions, institutions, and ways of living together of a group of people;

▶ How individuals learn the elements of their culture through interactions with other members of the culture group.

PRODUCTS EARLY GRADES

Learners demonstrate understanding by...

▶ Presenting a "compare and contrast" chart demonstrating the similarities and differences between two or more cultural groups...

National Curriculum Standards for Social Studies, pp. 27, 29.

Procedures

▶ Select an American Indian cultural group living in your state or region of the country.

▶ Identify where this people lived historically and where its members live today. Locate their home, both then and now, on a map of the United States.

▶ Divide the class into groups and have each group conduct research for information about a different aspect of the people's historical culture and way of life (e.g., language, art, music, legends, homes, lifestyle).

▶ Record information from research and prepare information for sharing with the class.

▶ Group share. Discussion questions: *How are these aspects of culture unique to this region or area of the country?* (Example: certain products of culture are made of materials found only in this region of the country) *What can we learn about this people from these aspects of culture? How are these aspects of culture similar to or different from the students' cultures? How are they familiar to and different from the Navajo culture as presented in the book?*

▶ Identify the location of the Navajo Reservation on a map of the United States. Compare its location to that of the American Indian people researched by the students, considering landforms, climate, elevation, etc. Use Google Earth or another online tool to show students this region as it exists today.

▶ As a class, research one aspect of traditional Navajo culture, such as language, art, music, legends, homes, or lifestyle to compare with that of the American Indian people the class has researched. (Check this Navajo Nation website for information: www.discovernavajo.com). Discussion questions: *What can we learn about the two groups from comparing aspects of their culture? How are the two peoples similar? How are they different?*

▶ Close the activity by having students write a paragraph or develop a chart summarizing the similarities and differences in the traditional cultures of the Navajo and the American Indian people they have researched.

Class Activity 2
Exploring the Colorado Plateau

NCSS Curriculum Standard

❸ PEOPLE, PLACES, AND ENVIRONMENTS

KNOWLEDGE EARLY GRADES

Learners will understand...

▸ Physical and human characteristics of the...region, and the interactions of people in these places with the environment.

PROCESSES EARLY GRADES

Learners will be able to...

▸ Investigate relationships among people and places, and environments in the...region,...through the use of atlases, data bases, charts, graphs, maps, and geospatial technologies.

PRODUCTS EARLY GRADES

Learners demonstrate understanding by....

▸ Creating illustrations and composing answers to geographic questions about people, places, and environments.

National Curriculum Standards for Social Studies, 35, 36, 37.

Procedures

▸ Share that the setting of the story—the Colorado Plateau Region of the Southwestern United States, which covers parts of Colorado, Arizona, New Mexico, and Utah—is important to the mood and feeling of the story. John has never lived away from the Navajo Reservation in the Colorado Plateau. His grandfather, upon returning from the war, saw the beautiful canyon floor and thought, "I'm never leaving again." The author shares this landform region with the reader through both words and illustrations. Students can use these parts of the story to begin an exploration of the plateau as a landform.

▸ Begin by rereading the story, this time highlighting the words and illustrations that describe the plateau region. As the story is reread, students identify features of a plateau as they are mentioned (e.g., *piñon trees, towering walls of the canyon, river winding below*) or illustrated (e.g., flat-topped mountains, little vegetation) and include them in a class chart titled, "Features of the Colorado Plateau." After reading, the children

can research the Colorado Plateau for information to add to the chart. (See the U.S. Geological Survey (USGS) website, *Land Use History of the Colorado Plateau*: http://cpluhna.nau.edu/)

▸ When the chart is completed with an accurate and correct listing of features found on the Colorado Plateau, students can, as closure for the activity, create drawings of the Colorado Plateau. Drawings should include several of the features listed on the class chart. Students can also compare and contrast the features of the plateau to landforms in their own region. Classrooms equipped with computer projection equipment can view areas of the Navajo reservation today on Google Images, including the breathtaking Canyon de Chelly, which could have been Grandfather's "beautiful canyon floor."

▸ To extend the activity, the teacher can show a map of the Colorado Plateau to the students and point out that not only the Navajo Indians, but other peoples, such as the Hopi, the Paiute, and the Havasupai, have lived in this area for hundreds of years. Ask students to consider how, in the past, these groups of people were able to live on the plateau? *How did they adapt to and interact with their environment? What were their homes like? What did they eat? Did they use plants from the environment? How did they make their living?*

Students make inferences based on their knowledge of the Plateau region and then research to check if their ideas were correct. (For information on the people of the Colorado Plateau, see the USGS website, http://cpluhna.nau.edu/)

Reading Activities

These activities can help to meet the following Reading and Language Standards of the Common Core State Standards for English Language Arts (Grade 4):

READING: LITERATURE—GRADE 4
Key Ideas and Details
1. Refer to details and examples in a text when explaining what the text says explicitly and when drawing inferences from the text.
2. Determine a theme of a story, drama, or poem from details in the text; summarize the text.

READING: FOUNDATIONAL SKILLS—GRADE 4
Phonics and Word Recognition
3. Know and apply grade-level phonics and word analysis skills in decoding words.
    (a) Use combined knowledge of all letter-sound correspondences, syllabication patterns, and morphology (e.g., roots and affixes) to read accurately unfamiliar multisyllabic words in context and out of context.

LANGUAGE—GRADE 4
Conventions of Standard English
2. Demonstrate command of the conventions of standard English capitalization, punctuation, and spelling when writing.
    (b) Use commas and quotation marks to mark direct speech and quotations from a text.

Vocabulary Acquisition and Use
4. Determine or clarify the meaning of unknown and multiple-meaning words and phrases based on *grade 4 reading and content*, choosing flexibly from a range of strategies.
    (a) Use context (e.g., definitions, examples, or restatements in text) as a clue to the meaning of a word or phrase.
5. Demonstrate understanding of figurative language, word relationships, and nuances in word meanings.
    (a) Explain the meaning of simple similes and metaphors (e.g., "as pretty as a picture") in context.

Common Core State Standards for English Language Arts & Literacy in History/Social Studies, Science, and Technical Subjects, p. 12 (Reading Literature); p. 17 (Foundational Skills); pp. 28, 29 (Language).

Inferences

▶ Help the students to draw inferences about the characters from details and examples in the text. *What can you infer about how John is feeling at the beginning of the story from reading the following sentences?*

"John dug his toe deeper into the dirt."
"John's shoulder sagged."

What did you already know that helped you make this inference? What details from the story helped you make this inference?

What can you infer about Grandfather's feelings for John from reading the following sentences from the story?

"Grandfather's soft, brown eyes disappeared in the wrinkles of a smile."

"Grandfather sat down and began to speak gently in Navajo."

What did you already know that helped you make this inference?

What details from the story helped you make this inference?

Vocabulary

▸ Students understand the meaning of 12 words within the context in which they are used in the story:

skidding	faint
bleat	bulletin
fluent	platoon
sacred	measure
corridor	accuracy
recruits	broadcasting

▸ Students practice putting the words into categories according to their use in the story (e.g., Military Words, Verbs, Nouns, Adjectives).

▸ Students explain other meanings for words with multiple meanings (i.e., faint, measure, bulletin).

Phonics and Word Recognition

▸ Students use affixes, including Greek and Latin affixes, to read multi-syllabic words in and out of context. Students can read the following sentences containing multi-syllabic words with affixes from the story or practice with a list.

*"So far the Japanese had been able to **intercept** and **decode** all American radio messages in only minutes."*

*"Behind a building at the other end of the field, another code talker sat under military guard waiting for my **transmission**."*

*"'**Receiving** steady machine gun fire. Request **reinforcements**.'"*

*"It took only seconds for me to speak into the **microphone** in Navajo code."*

▸ Students identify common affixes found in words from the story and explain the meaning of the root with the affix.

successful	bottomless
unbreakable	stillness
darkness	beautiful
midsummer	enlisted

Punctuation

▸ Students can practice the correct use of commas and quotation marks to show direct speech by placing them correctly in dialogue from *The Unbreakable Code*.

In our story, Grandfather and John often spoke to one another. Remember there are special punctuation rules when writing conversation that make it easier for the reader to know who is speaking. Commas and quotation marks are used to show the exact words someone says. Add commas and quotation marks to the sentences below to show the exact words stated by each character.

Grandfather said You're going to be all right.

I'm not going John said.

But you weren't seventeen said John.

John whispered I'll probably forget how to speak Navajo.

He said You don't know what it's like there!

Writing

▸ Students can also practice writing dialogue that might occur between Grandfather and John the next summer when John returns from Minnesota.

Multiple Meanings: Frequently Confused Words

▸ Use these sentences summarizing John's feelings to explain the difference between frequently confused words:

*He did not want to go to Minnesota. Grandfather did not know what it was like to go **there**.*

He wanted to stay with Grandfather. The reservation was **their** home.

In the end, he learned what the important things in life were and that **they're** with him wherever he goes.

▸ Similar practice can be done with **to, too** and **two** using examples from the story.

▸ Students can then practice writing sentences showing correct usage of these words.

Figurative Language

▸ Students can explain the meaning of simple similes used in the story. They can identify each simile and what is being described.

"The river full of late-summer rain looked like a silver thread winding through his grandfather's farm."

"The sounds wove up and down, in and out, as warm and familiar as the patterns of one of Grandmother's Navajo blankets."

"Suddenly Grandfather's face looked as creased and battered as the canyon walls behind him."

▸ As follow up practice, students could write two to four sentences using simple similes.

▸ You could also use the following sentence to introduce another type of figurative language used in the story: personification.

*"Out in the open, **the stars danced above me** and the tumbleweeds blew by my feet as I ran."*

Other Recommended Books for the Fourth Grade Classroom

The following books can be used to teach the nine social studies themes other than **CULTURE** (Theme 1, which is the principal focus of Activity 1). All the books can be used to meet Standard 1 of the Common Core Reading Standards for Literature (Grade 4): "Refer to details and examples in a text when explaining what the text says explicitly and when drawing inferences from the text." As teachers review the books, they can use the chart of standards on pp. 8–9 to develop strategies for meeting other Common Core Reading Standards for Literature in Grade 4 when they use the books in class.

❷ TIME, CONTINUITY, AND CHANGE

Neil Waldman, *They Came From the Bronx: How the Buffalo Were Saved from Extinction* (Honesdale, PA: Boyd Mills Press, 2001)

In 1905, conservationists from the Bronx Zoo, concerned about the small number of buffalo, began "seed herds" to be relocated in the West. This book was a Notable Social Studies Trade Book in 2002.
QUESTION FOR EXPLORATION: What caused events described in the book?

❸ PEOPLE, PLACES, AND ENVIRONMENTS

Lynne Cherry, *A River Ran Wild* (San Diego: Harcourt Brace, 1992)

The story of the Nashua River in Massachusetts is used to show change over time and the negative effects of human-environmental interaction. This book was a Notable Social Studies Trade Book in 1993.
QUESTION FOR EXPLORATION: How do people change the environment, and how does the environment influence human activity?

❹ INDIVIDUAL DEVELOPMENT AND IDENTITY

Kathleen Krull, *Harvesting Hope: The Story of Cesar Chavez* (San Diego: Harcourt Children's Books, 2003)
Cesar Chavez grows from a shy boy to the man who led migrant farm workers to march for better working conditions and better pay. This book was a Notable Social Studies Trade Book in 2004, and also received a Carter G. Woodson Honor in the same year.
QUESTION FOR EXPLORATION: How can institutions help to meet individual needs and promote the common good?

❺ INDIVIDUALS, GROUPS, AND INSTITUTIONS

Linda Arms White, *I Could Do That! Esther Morris Gets Women the Vote* (New York: Farrar Straus Giroux, Melanie Kroupa Books: 2005)
Hat maker, wife, mother, pioneer, and activist, Esther Morris worked to get the vote for women in Wyoming. Through the mantra of her life—I could do that!—she shows how an individual can work to bring positive change. This book was a Notable Social Studies Trade Book in 2006.
QUESTION FOR EXPLORATION: How do the groups to which I belong influence me, and how do I influence them?

❻ POWER, AUTHORITY, AND GOVERNANCE

Ellen Levine, *Henry's Freedom Box: A True Story from the Underground Railroad* (New York: Scholastic Press, 2007)
Henry Brown dreams of freedom. This book, which received a 2008 Caldecott Honor, is the true story of how Henry escaped from slavery by mailing himself to freedom inside a wooden crate. This book was a Notable Social Studies Trade Book in 2008.
QUESTION FOR EXPLORATION: What questions are important to ask about power?

❼ PRODUCTION, DISTRIBUTION, AND CONSUMPTION

Maribeth Boelts, *Those Shoes* (Somerville, MA: Candlewick Press, 2007)
Jeremy wants a new pair of shoes—those shoes—black high tops with two white stripes. Grandma explains that what he needs is more important than what he wants and he needs new winter boots, not expensive shoes. Jeremy learns an important lesson about what is truly important in his life.
QUESTION FOR EXPLORATION: Why can't people have everything they want?

❽ SCIENCE, TECHNOLOGY, AND SOCIETY

Wendie Old, *To Fly: The Story of the Wright Brothers* (New York: Houghton Mifflin, Clarion Books, 2002)
This story is about the Wright Brothers and the way in which they worked together to solve the problems and overcome the obstacles that kept so many others from gaining the first heavier-than-air-manned flight. This book was a Notable Social Studies Trade Book in 2003.
QUESTION FOR EXPLORATION: What are examples of science and technology that have impacted individuals and society?

❾ GLOBAL CONNECTIONS

Margy Burns Knight, *Talking Walls* (Gardiner, ME: Tilbury House, 1992)
People throughout time and in different places built walls. This book explores the reasons why people build walls and also illustrates the connections we can make to others through learning about their walls.
QUESTION FOR EXPLORATION: How are people, places, and environments connected around the world?

⑩ CIVIC IDEALS AND PRACTICES

Eileen Christelow, *Vote* (New York: Houghton Mifflin, Clarion, 2003)

Angela's mother is running for mayor. Through her campaign, Angela learns all about the election process and why it is important to vote. This book was a Notable Social Studies Trade Book in 2004.

QUESTION FOR EXPLORATION: What are civic practices? 🌐

The books cited in this chapter are recommended for their value in implementing the National Curriculum Standards for Social Studies and the Common Core State Standards for English Language Arts in Grade 4. They can also be used to help to meet the following standards of the national Standards for the English Language Arts published in 1996 by the International Reading Association and National Council of Teachers of English.

2 Students read a wide range of literature from many periods in many genres to build an understanding of many dimensions (e.g., philosophical, ethical, aesthetic) of human experience.

3 Students apply a wide range of strategies to comprehend, interpret, evaluate, and appreciate texts. They draw on their prior experience, their interactions with other readers and writers, their knowledge of word meaning and of other texts, their word identification strategies, and their understanding of textual features (e.g., sound-letter correspondence, sentence structure, context, graphics)

9 Students develop an understanding of and respect for diversity in language use, patterns, and dialects across cultures, ethnic groups, geographic regions, and social roles.

International Reading Association (IRA) and National Council of Teachers of English (NCTE), *Standards for the English Language Arts* (Newark, DE and Urbana, IL: IRA and NCTE, 1996): 21, 22, and 29.

11 Fifth Grade

Joan Brodsky Schur

Sarah, Plain and Tall
Written by Patricia MacLachlan
New York: Harper, 1985

In spare and poetic language, *Sarah, Plain and Tall* describes the hardships and rewards of a pioneer family on the Great Plains. It won the Newbery Medal in 1986. The story is narrated by Anna, who lives on a farm with her younger brother, Caleb, and their widowed father, Jacob. As the novel opens, Caleb asks Anna to recount her memories about their mother, who died just after giving birth to him. Jacob's decision to advertise for a mail order bride from back east provides the impetus for the story. Sarah is the respondent who agrees to live with Anna's family for one month before she decides whether or not to leave behind her home on the sea-sprayed coast of Maine for the life of a farmer's wife on the Great Plains. Will Caleb and Anna succeed in making Sarah feel welcome? Will Sarah overcome her homesickness and adjust to life in a new environment? Will their father accept that the "plain and tall" Sarah is a strong-willed and independent woman? The resolution of the story is Sarah's decision to stay.

Students can easily identify with several aspects of this story, from the yearning to make a broken family whole again, to the necessity of pulling up one's roots and seeking happiness in a new location. The author never names the prairie state of Sarah's adopted

Social Studies Standards Theme
❸ PEOPLE, PLACES, AND ENVIRONMENTS

Other Related Theme
❷ TIME, CONTINUITY, AND CHANGE

Common Core Standards
READING: LITERATURE — GRADE 5
Key Ideas and Details
1. Quote accurately from a text when explaining what the text says explicitly and when drawing inferences from the text.
2. Determine a theme of a story, drama, or poem from details in the text, including how characters in a story or drama respond to challenges or how the speaker in a poem reflects upon a topic; summarize the text.
3. Compare and contrast two or more characters, settings, or events in a story or drama, drawing on specific details in the text (e.g., how characters interact).

LANGUAGE—GRADE 5
Vocabulary Acquisition and Use
4. Determine or clarify the meaning of unknown and multiple-meaning words and phrases based on *grade 5 reading and content*, choosing flexibly from a range of strategies.

WRITING—GRADE 5
Text Types and Purposes
2. Write informative/explanatory texts to examine a topic and convey ideas and information clearly.

Production and Distribution of Writing
4. Produce clear and coherent writing in which the development and organization are appropriate to task, purpose, and audience.

homestead, nor does she date the events in the novel, but Patricia MacLachlan herself was born in Wyoming and grew up in Minnesota. We can roughly date the events in the novel and its sequel by the appearance of the railroad and a phonograph, which became a popular invention beginning in the late 1870s. In her Newbery acceptance speech MacLachlan wrote, "My mother told me early on about the real Sarah who came from the coast of Maine to the prairie to become a wife and mother to a close family member." In the novel's sequel *Skylark*, Sarah's new family faces a drought and its consequences.

Scholastic, which publishes the book in the school market under license from HarperCollins, recommends *Sarah, Plain and Tall* for Grades 4-6, and lists the book as suitable for young learners between the ages of 8 and 12. Students in Grade 5 are typically at the upper end of this age range, and the book can be used in English classes at earlier grade levels.[1]

For teaching social studies, the novel can be a valuable enhancement for fifth grade classes studying U.S. history or historical geography, especially subjects such as the Westward Movement, and historical patterns of migration in the United States. The activities outlined in this chapter treat the novel as a starting point for studying migration patterns of the kind recommended in the social studies standards as suitable for students at the middle levels (grades 5 and above). Teachers can use the book to reinforce concepts in Theme 3, **PEOPLE, PLACES, AND ENVIRONMENTS**, of the National Curriculum Standards for Social Studies: "Learners examine where people, places, and resources are located, why they are there, and why this matters."[2] Descriptions in the novel contrast sea-coastal New England with the land-locked plains. While Sarah keeps yearning for the geographical region she left behind, the children help her to see their similarities: "There is no sea here. But the land rolls a little like the sea."

Theme 3, **PEOPLE, PLACES, AND ENVIRONMENTS** also encompasses the study of demographics. Students learn about "the study of the relationships between human populations in different locations and geographic phenomena," as well as patterns of demographic change and human settlement, the roles of different kinds of population centers, and the "push" and "pull" factors that influence migration.[3] From a careful reading of *Sarah, Plain and Tall,* students can infer the push/pull factors that impelled Sarah to move: she was headed for spinsterhood in New England and desired both a family and an independent lifestyle. While MacLachlan does not tell us why Jacob's family moved to the Great Plains, teachers can ask students to draw on what they have learned about the Homestead Act and the dehumanization of industrial labor in the East to formulate hypothetical reasons for their migration west. In the final social studies activity, students analyze U.S. Census records from 1880 and make deductions about the effects of gender imbalance in different regions of the United States following the Civil War.

This research enables students to accomplish the learning expectations for Theme 2 of the social studies standards, **TIME, CONTINUITY, AND CHANGE**, that emphasize the importance of using primary sources.[4]

As a work of inspiring literature, *Sarah, Plain and Tall* can be used to teach plot development, characterization, symbolism, and creating writing.

Teaching Physical Geography

NCSS Curriculum Standard

❸ PEOPLE, PLACES, AND ENVIRONMENTS

KNOWLEDGE MIDDLE GRADES

▶ Learners will understand....
The theme of people, places, and environments involves the study of the relationships between human populations in different locations and geographic phenomena such as climate, vegetation, and natural resources;

▶ Concepts such as: location, region, place and migration, as well as human and physical systems;

▶ Past and present changes in physical systems, such as seasons, climate, and weather....

PROCESSES MIDDLE GRADES

Learners will be able to....

▶ Ask and find answers to geographic questions related to regions, nations, and the world in the past and present;

▶ Research, organize, analyze, synthesize, and evaluate information from atlases, data bases, grid systems, charts, graphs, maps, geospatial technologies, and other tools to interpret relationships among geographic factors and historic events.

National Curriculum Standards for Social Studies, pp. 35, 36.

Procedure

▶ Guide students as they use their atlases and outline maps of the United States to research and label every state on the Great Plains. How do geographers define "prairie"? MacLachlan contrasts the seacoast of Maine to the landlocked plains, but originally the Great Plains were covered by a vast inland sea, deposits of which are evident in its rock strata. Before European colonization, the Great Plains covered about one quarter of the North American continent. Only in a few places are the original high grasses of the prairie still intact today. How did the desire to plow and farm disrupt the ecosystem that had supported native peoples for thousands of years?

▶ Ask students to use their atlases to contrast the climate of New England and that of the Great Plains today. How do mountain ranges affect the continental climate of the plains? How do sea currents affect the climate of coastal New England? What factors make the sea life of the Gulf of Maine one of the most biologically diverse and productive ecosystems in the world? What decisions affecting these regions are pending today? What is at stake?

▶ Using their atlases, challenge students to complete the following activities:

- Measure the distance that Sarah traveled from (let's say) Portland, Maine to St. Cloud, Minnesota. What proportion of the width of the continental United States did Sarah cross?

- Find three different routes that Sarah might have taken to travel from Portland to St. Cloud in approximately 1880 using overland trails, river, lake, sea, canal, and rail. Compare her journey to options for making that journey today.

- Find the latitude of Portland, Maine and St. Cloud, Minnesota and compare them. What predictions can students make about weather patterns, based on latitude?

- In the novel, Sarah loves to sketch. Supply students with the materials to make a sketchbook of the contrasting flora and fauna found in the Northeast and Great Plains. As they read, assign students to keep two lists of what grows and lives in each of the two habitats. Examples include:

  Coastal Gulf of Maine

  Kittiwake, flounder, bluefish, whales, sea birds, seal, moon snail, gulls, scallop, sea clam, oyster, razor clam, conch shell, sand dunes, rock cliffs, pine, spruce, roses, nasturtiums, dahlias, columbine, blue flax.

  Great Plains

  Gophers, woodchuck, marsh hawk, meadowlark, turkey buzzards, crows, killdeer, chickens, cows, goats, sheep, Indian paintbrush, tumble weeds, dandelions, corn, zinnias, marigolds, prairie violets, wild roses, wild feverfew.

- Direct students to sketch, research and label one item they find for each environment. What does the plant or animal need to survive and how does it contribute to the ecosystem to which it belongs? For example, gophers provided a necessary service on the Great Plains, digging deep among its dense and intertwined roots, aerating the soil and enabling water to percolate downward.

- Assign students to design a state flag, quarter, or license plate based on what they have learned from the novel about the geography of Maine and Minnesota. Then, have students investigate and compare their design to the existing flag, quarter or license plate for either state, responding to the question: which best reflects the geography of the state—the one you created or the real one? How? Useful sites include: www.netstate. com/state_flags.htm and www.usmint.gov/mint_ programs/50sq_program/?action=designs_50sq

- How do humans adapt to challenging physical conditions? Tell students to find examples from the novel. For example, there is harsh weather in both Maine and on the Great Plains. Also, New England fishing villages were clustered on the coastline, but on the flat and sparsely- settled prairie, Sarah needs to learn to ride a horse and buggy.

Teaching Push and Pull Factors

NCSS Curriculum Standard

❸ PEOPLE, PLACES, AND ENVIRONMENTS

QUESTIONS FOR EXPLORATION MIDDLE GRADES

▶ What "push/pull" factors influence the migration of peoples?
▶ How are people, ideas, and products diffused across the earth?

KNOWLEDGE MIDDLE GRADES

Learners will understand...

▶ Concepts such as: location, region, place, and migration, as well as human and physical systems;
▶ Patterns of demographic and political change, and cultural diffusion in the past and present (e.g., changing national boundaries, migration, and settlement, and the diffusion of and changes in customs and ideas).

PROCESSES MIDDLE GRADES

Learners will be able to...

▶ Identify and interpret "push" and "pull" factors involved in the migrations of people in this nation and other parts of the world.

PRODUCTS MIDDLE GRADES

Learners demonstrate understanding by....

▶ Graphing patterns of human migration in a selected place on the globe.

National Curriculum Standards for Social Studies, pp. 34, 35, 36, 37.

▶ Ask students to research when each state on the Great Plains entered the Union. What were the push/pull factors that drew Anglo and European settlers into the region? How did transportation impede or facilitate their journeys at different times in American history?

▶ Nearly every American family has the story of a journey to tell: a reason why they left one place and traveled to another. Some were immigrant journeys to America, others were dislocations or relocations within the United States — such as the enforced exile of native peoples in the face of expanding white settlement, or the journey of African American families who fled the South during the years of the Great Migration. MacLachlan based her novel on such a family story. Ask class members to interview a member of the family or a family friend about a move that

they or their ancestors made. What were the push and pull factors that led to the migration? What was similar and different about the new geographical environment to the one left behind? What helped the family adjust?

▶ Use the "mail order bride system" to teach about the relationship of geography to demographics in 1880, using the 1880 U.S. Census, which can be downloaded at **www.census.gov/prod/www/ abs/decennial/1880.html**. Volume V1-03 includes "The Population of the United States Classified by Sex." Ask students to evaluate which states or territories had a surplus of men, and which lacked women. In order to help students visualize the imbalance reported in the raw data of the census, ask students to make bar graphs that show these differentials. For example, assign students to make a bar graph that shows the male and female population in each of three Eastern Seaboard states (Maine, Rhode Island, and Connecticut) and in each of three states or territories of the West (Minnesota, Dakota, and Wyoming). Students can thus grasp more easily why men like Sarah's father had to seek brides back East.

▸ Next ask students to access the Tables of Occupations to figure out the likely occupations of men in need of wives. Finally, students can analyze the table entitled Influence of Physical Features upon the Distribution of Population, which analyzes U.S. population by region. (All of these tables are surprisingly easy to use.) Students should then take on the role of demographers writing a census report in which they analyze the causes and effects of shifting patterns of settlement within the United States.

▸ You can also set up a role-play for a Mail Order Bride using data from the U.S. Census of 1880 in which half the class is assigned to imagine themselves as men seeking a bride in 1880. The "men" write advertisements for a mail order bride in which they describe an occupation (e.g. farmer, miner, rancher), the state or territory in which they live, and why they would make attractive mates. Assign each "woman" in the class to respond with a letter to one of the men. The women should explain their prospects for marriage and work where they currently live (as teacher, factory worker, caregiver, and wife), and why they would make desirable mates.

Reading and Writing Activities

These activities can help to meet the following Standards for Reading Literature, Language, and Writing from the Common Core State Standards for English Language Arts (Grade 5)

READING: LITERATURE—GRADE 5
Key Ideas and Details
1. Quote accurately from a text when explaining what the text says explicitly and when drawing inferences from the text.
2. Determine a theme of a story, drama, or poem from details in the text, including how characters in a story or drama respond to challenges or how the speaker in a poem reflects upon a topic; summarize the text.
3. Compare and contrast two or more characters, settings, or events in a story or drama, drawing on specific details in the text (e.g., how characters interact).

LANGUAGE STANDARDS—GRADE 5
Vocabulary Acquisition and Use
4. Determine or clarify the meaning of unknown and multiple-meaning words and phrases based on *grade 5 reading and content*, choosing flexibly from a range of strategies.

WRITING—GRADE 5
Text Types and Purposes
2. Write informative/explanatory texts to examine a topic and convey ideas and information clearly.

Production and Distribution of Writing
4. Produce clear and coherent writing in which the development and organization are appropriate to task, purpose, and audience.

Common Core State Standards for English Language Arts & Literacy in History/Social Studies, Science, and Technical Subjects, p. 12 (Reading Literature); p. 29 (Language); pp. 20, 21 (Writing).

Inferring Theme

▶ Learners can become engaged in making inferences and citing from the text when given the right assignment. One task that is both enjoyable and challenging is to ask students to create their own chapter headings for a novel that does not have any, such as *Sarah, Plain and Tall*. To do this, students must first identify the main idea of each chapter. For example, before learners read chapter 1, explain that you will ask them, when reading is completed, to describe what this chapter is about, and that the expectation will be for each of them to respond in a single sentence. Also explain that you will expect each of them to supply one quotation from the book that backs up their summary statement. At the appropriate moment, get responses (including quotations) from learners and list them where all can see. Then discuss which summary statement might be the "best." One possible response: This chapter is about the death of Caleb and Anna's "Mama" and the possibility of their getting a new "mother." A supporting quotation would be, "I looked at the long dirt road that crawled across the plains, remembering the morning that Mama had died, cruel and sunny." Explain to learners how this activity helps them to make inferences about that chapter's main idea. Then work with learners to create a chapter title based on the main idea. This strategy can be applied with any or all of the other chapters in the book. A final list of all main ideas/chapter titles could serve as a summary of the book's contents.

Analyzing Plot

▶ Help students to make a graphic organizer (see Figure 1) of the rising and falling action in *Sarah, Plain and Tall*. The "plot line" should start with the exposition (introduction to the characters, setting and situation), slope up with the rising action as suspense builds, peak at the climax which is the highest point of tension in the novel and the turning point, then start to slope downward with the falling action as the situation moves to its resolution. Encourage classroom debate about where students think different events belong along the "plot line."

Vocabulary Relating to People, Places and Environments

▶ The following ten words can help fulfill the Grade 5 Language Standard cited above for determining and clarifying the meaning of unknown and multiple-meaning words and phrases

Hearthstone	Prairie
Colt	Stalls (horse stalls)
Windbreak	Paddock
Dune	Lantern
Plow	Squall

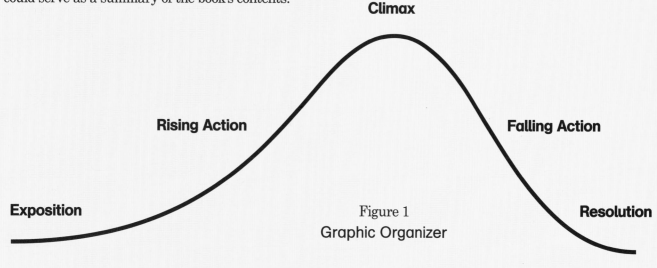

Climax

Rising Action

Falling Action

Exposition

Figure 1
Graphic Organizer

Resolution

Understanding Character

▶ Ask students to:

- Make a list of characters in the novel and explain their significance, including the animals that are given names. *(Main Characters: Anna, Caleb, Papa [Jacob], Sarah. Supporting Characters: Maggie and Matthew [neighbors from Tennessee] and their children Rose and Violet, William, Sarah's brother. Dogs: Nick and Lottie. Horses: Jack and Old Bess. Cat: Seal.)*

- Explain why Sarah accepted Jacob's invitation to move West to be his wife. *(Up until now Sarah has lived with her brother as mistress of their home. Sarah will cede this position when the wife of her newly-wed brother arrives to take the reins. Sarah could live with one of her aunts, also in a subservient role. Her prospects of finding a mate and having a home of her own in Maine seem slim ["...the sea is as far east as I can go. My choice, as you can see, is limited."]. As a woman who likes to be independent, Sarah therefore opts to move west.)*

- Describe how Sarah extends herself to the children, even before she arrives. *(She sends them a book about sea birds; she encloses a drawing of her cat; she lets them know that she sings.)*

- List the ways in which Caleb, Anna and Jacob help to make Sarah feel at home. *(They reassure her in various ways that the prairie is not so different from the sea. Papa makes a "dune" out of hay, etc.)*

- Compare Papa's character to Sarah's, including similarities and differences. *(They are both independent people who rise to the challenges of life; Sarah brings to life a greater sensitivity to beauty, as exemplified by her sketching.)*

- Describe the first indications we have that Papa also likes Sarah. *(He picks wild daisies for her and later roses.)*

- Explain how we know that Jacob accepts Sarah's independent streak? *(After their argument Papa lets Sarah ride into town alone with the horse of her choice. He admires her "can do" spirit and know-how in helping him to fix the roof.)*

- Describe how Sarah overcomes being homesick. *(She learns that people can be more important than places; she uses her artwork to recreate images of her cherished sea.)*

Writing an Essay about Sarah's Character

▶ Throughout the novel we learn a great deal about Sarah's character. Assign students to write an essay on the following topic: *Describe three aspects of Sarah's character. Discuss whether or not each character trait is a strength or weakness in helping her to adapt to her new environment on the prairie.*

How to Scaffold the Pre-Writing Phase

▶ Explain to students that characterization is the method authors use to develop a fictional character. MacLachlan tells us about Sarah through her appearance, actions, words, and how others respond to Sarah. For example, Sarah describes herself as "plain and tall" and says that she is "not mild mannered."

▶ Ask students to fill in the following chart by providing examples from the novel.

HOW WE LEARN ABOUT SARAH	EXAMPLE FROM THE NOVEL	ADJECTIVE THAT DESCRIBES SARAH
Sarah's appearance		
What Sarah writes or says		
What Sarah does – her actions		
How others respond to Sarah		

▶ To prepare to write essays, ask students to fill in the following chart.

ADJECTIVE THAT DESCRIBES SARAH (CHARACTER TRAIT)	EXAMPLE AND PAGE NUMBER	ADVANTAGE OR DISADVANTAGE
1.		
2.		
3.		

Singing as a Symbol in the Novel

▸ The novel opens with Caleb's question, "Did Mama sing every day?" Throughout the novel singing is a *symbol* that represents the happiness that Anna and Caleb lost with the death of their mother, and the happiness they hope to regain through Sarah. As students read, ask them to take special note of every reference to singing (and every song). Then ask them to explain and/or write about why singing is an important symbol that explains the meaning of this story.

Creative Writing Assignments

▸ The author does not include the advertisement Papa places in the newspaper requesting responses from a suitable bride. Using what you know about Papa's family and his farm, write the advertisement yourself. What information should you include? Can you phrase your advertisement artfully such that it would entice a bride to come? How will you format the ad to make it noticeable and appealing?

▸ Both Anna and Jacob evidently write to Sarah, but we never get to read their letters. The author only includes what Sarah wrote in response to their questions. Write the letter that either Anna or Jacob wrote to Sarah. Use proper formatting for a letter.

▸ We know that Sarah corresponds with her brother William. Imagine what Sarah writes to him and envision the accompanying sketches she sends east in order to describe her new life on the prairie. Now write the letter she would write and submit it with your accompanying sketches.

Other Recommended Books for the Fifth Grade Classroom

The following books can be used to teach the nine social studies themes other than Theme 3, **PEOPLE, PLACES, AND ENVIRONMENTS** (which is the principal focus of the above Activities). All books can be used to meet Standard 1 of the Common Core State Standards for Reading Literature for Grade 5: "Quote accurately from a text when explaining what the text says explicitly and when drawing inferences from a text." As teachers review the books, they can use the chart of standards on pp. 8–9 to develop strategies for meeting other Common Core Standards for Reading

Literature in Grade 5 when they use the books in class.

❶ CULTURE

Gloria Whelan, *Homeless Bird* (New York: HarperCollins, 2000)
Set in contemporary India, this novel tells the story of Koly, a child bride who is widowed and left without means of support until she learns to sew. This book was a National Book Award Winner in 2000.
QUESTION FOR EXPLORATION: How do cultures solve common problems related to food, shelter, and social interactions?

❷ TIME, CONTINUITY, AND CHANGE

E.L. Konigsburg, *A Proud Taste for Scarlet and Miniver* (New York: Simon and Schuster, Atheneum, 2001)

An engaging fictional account of the life of Eleanor of Aquitaine, one of the most powerful and influential women of the Middle Ages.

QUESTION FOR EXPLORATION: What connections are there between the past and present?

❹ INDIVIDUAL DEVELOPMENT AND IDENTITY

Christopher Paul Curtis, *Bud, Not Buddy* (New York: Random House, Yearling, 1999)

Bud is an orphaned ten-year-old who leaves his foster home in search of his supposed father and discovers many things along his journey to self discovery. This book won the 2000 Newbery Medal.

QUESTION FOR EXPLORATION: How does personal motivation impact individual development and identity?

❺ INDIVIDUALS, GROUPS, AND INSTITUTIONS

Sydney Taylor, *All of a Kind Family* (New York: Bantam Doubleday Dell, 1984)

The classic story of five sisters growing up on New York's Lower East Side and the ways in which their Jewish heritage helps them to surmount a variety of hardships.

QUESTION FOR EXPLORATION: How do groups and institutions influence individuals and society?

❻ POWER, AUTHORITY, AND GOVERNANCE

Andrea Davis Pinkney, *Dear Mr. President: Letters from a Slave Girl* (New York: Winslow, 2001)

In this fictional correspondence between a 12-year-old enslaved girl and President Lincoln, Lettie urges the president to free the slaves.

QUESTION FOR EXPLORATION: What are the purposes and functions of government?

❼ PRODUCTION, DISTRIBUTION, AND CONSUMPTION

Susan Campbell Bartoletti, *Growing Up in Coal Country* (New York: Houghton Mifflin Company, 1999)

The hardships faced by children and adults in the coalmines at the turn of the last century are described through vivid photographs, oral history, and primary source documents.

QUESTION FOR EXPLORATION: How does the availability of resources influence decisions about production, distribution, and consumption?

❽ SCIENCE, TECHNOLOGY, AND SOCIETY

Martha E. Kendall, *The Erie Canal* (Washington, DC: National Geographic, 2008)

This is the story of the building of the canal that linked New York City to the Great Lakes, and transformed American society in the process.

QUESTION FOR EXPLORATION: How can science and technology be used to address societal problems or issues?

❾ GLOBAL CONNECTIONS

Pam Munoz Ryan, *Esperanza Rising* (New York: Scholastic, 2002)

Esperanza and her family are forced to flee Mexico in the 1930s and subsequently face problems adjusting to life in California's agricultural heartland. This book was a Notable Social Studies Trade Book in 2001.

QUESTION FOR EXPLORATION: What types of global connections exist in the community, state, region, and nation?

❿ CIVIC IDEALS AND PRACTICES

Karen Hesse, *Witness* (New York: Scholastic, 2001)

A cast of characters living in Vermont in 1924 comes to life in verse, as town members confront the power of prejudice and the Ku Klux Klan.

QUESTION FOR EXPLORATION: How are civic ideals translated into practice? ▨

NOTES

1. Information about the grade levels for which Scholastic recommends the book is available at www.scholastic.com. Select the Teachers Site, enter the book's title in the search engine, and click on the book's cover for details. While the regular edition of the book is recommended for grades 4–6, other publications on the Scholastic site indicate that the book can be used as early as grade 3 and as late as grades 7 and 8.

   The Common Core State Standards for English Language Arts list the book as suitable for teaching English Language Arts in grades 2–3 (see National Governors Association Center for Best Practices and Council of Chief State School Officers, *Common Core State Standards for English Language Arts and Literacy in History/Social Studies, Science, and Technical Subjects* [Washington, D.C.: National Governors Association Center for Best Practices and Council of Chief State School Officers, 2010], 32). I consider the book to be above a typical Grade 2 level. MacLachlan's language is deceptively simple, reading like a prose poem in which what is unstated is often as important as what is stated. Thus an astute reader must make many inferences, sentence by sentence, to grasp the implications of what is written. The social studies activities suggested in this chapter also require the application of analytical thinking skills higher than those suitable for grades 2–3.

2. National Council for the Social Studies (NCSS), *National Curriculum Standards for Social Studies: A Framework for Teaching, Learning, and Assessment* (Silver Spring, MD: NCSS, 2010), 34.

3. *National Curriculum Standards for Social Studies: A Framework for Teaching, Learning, and Assessment*, 34-36.

4. See, for example, *ibid.*, p. 32 (Processes for Middle Grades) and p. 33 (Products for Middle Grades).

The books cited in this chapter are recommended for their value in implementing the National Curriculum Standards for Social Studies and the Common Core State Standards for English Language Arts in Grade 5. They can also be used to help to meet the following standards of the national Standards for the English Language Arts published in 1996 by the International Reading Association and National Council of Teachers of English.

2 Students read a wide range of literature from many periods in many genres to build an understanding of many dimensions (e.g., philosophical, ethical, aesthetic) of human experience.

3 Students apply a wide range of strategies to comprehend, interpret, evaluate, and appreciate texts. They draw on their prior experience, their interactions with other readers and writers, their knowledge of word meaning and of other texts, their word identification strategies, and their understanding of textual features (e.g., sound-letter correspondence, sentence structure, context, graphics)

6 Students apply knowledge of language structure, language conventions (e.g., spelling and punctuation), media techniques, figurative language, and genre to create, critique, and discuss print and nonprint texts.

International Reading Association (IRA) and National Council of Teachers of English (NCTE), *Standards for the English Language Arts* (Newark, DE and Urbana, IL: IRA and NCTE, 1996): 21, 22, and 26.

12 Bibliography
Additional Suggested Books
Meredith McGowan

The following list of books can be used to teach reading with the social studies standards. The list includes 20 suggested books for each of the grade levels from pre-K/K through Grade 5. Each book is matched with a suitable theme from the national social studies standards. The titles have been taken mainly from the following sources:

▸ The NCSS Lists of Notable Social Studies Trade Books for Young People for 2008, 2009, 2010
▸ The NCSS Carter Woodson Awards for 2008, 2009, 2010
▸ The Best Books of 2010, compiled by Sally Snyder, Nebraska Library Commission, Lincoln, Nebraska
▸ The Lincoln City Libraries, Lincoln, Nebraska collection, with corresponding reviews

Prekindergarten/Kindergarten

Ajmera, Maya, Sheila Kinkade, and Cynthia Pon. *Our Grandparents: A Global Album.* Watertown, MA: Charlesbridge, 2010. 32 pp.
❹ INDIVIDUAL DEVELOPMENT AND IDENTITY

Bruchac, Joseph. *My Father is Taller than a Tree.* Illus. by Wendy Halperin. New York: Penguin, Dial Books for Young Readers, 2010. Unp.
❹ INDIVIDUAL DEVELOPMENT AND IDENTITY

Cooper, Ilene. *Jake's Best Thumb.* Illus. by Claudio Munoz. New York: Penguin, Dutton Children's Books, 2008. 32 pp.
❹ INDIVIDUAL DEVELOPMENT AND IDENTITY

Cousins, Lucy. *I'm the Best.* Somerville, MA: Candlewick Press, 2010. Unp.
❺ INDIVIDUALS, GROUPS, AND INSTITUTIONS

Elya, Susan Middleton. *No More, Por Favor.* Illus. by David Walker. New York: Penguin, Putnam, 2010. 32 pp.
❸ PEOPLE, PLACES, AND ENVIRONMENTS

Glass, Julie. *A Dollar for Penny.* Illus. by Joy Allen. New York: Random House Books for Young Readers, 2000. Unp.
❼ PRODUCTION, DISTRIBUTION, AND CONSUMPTION

Hall, Michael. *My Heart is Like a Zoo.* New York: HarperCollins, Greenwillow, 2010. 32 pp.
❹ INDIVIDUAL DEVELOPMENT AND IDENTITY

Hoberman, Mary Ann. *Fathers, Mothers, Sisters, Brothers: A Collection of Family Poems.* Illus. by Marilyn Hafner. New York: Little, Brown & Company, 2009. 32 pp.
❺ INDIVIDUALS, GROUPS, AND INSTITUTIONS

Horacek, Petr. *Silly Suzy Goose.* Somerville, MA: Candlewick Press, 2006. 32 pp.
❺ INDIVIDUALS, GROUPS, AND INSTITUTIONS

Hudson, Cheryl Willis. *Hands Can.* Photographed by John-Francis Bourke. Somerville, MA: Candlewick, 2003. Unp.
❹ INDIVIDUAL DEVELOPMENT AND IDENTITY

Johnston, Tony. *My Abuelita.* Illus. by Yuyi Morales. Photographed by Tim O'Meara. San Diego: Harcourt Children's Books, 2009. 32 pp.
❶ CULTURE

Lyon, George Ella, Illus. by Vera Rosenberry. *Together.* New York: Orchard Books, 1989. Unp.
❹ INDIVIDUAL DEVELOPMENT AND IDENTITY

Morris, Ann. *Families.* New York: HarperCollins, 2000. 29 pp.
❾ GLOBAL CONNECTIONS

Nelson, Robin. *Home Then and Now.* Minneapolis, MN: Lerner Classroom, 2003. 24 pp.
❷ TIME, CONTINUITY, AND CHANGE

Pinkney, Jerry. *Three Little Kittens.* New York: Penguin, Dial Books for Young Readers, 2010. 32 pp.
❹ INDIVIDUAL DEVELOPMENT AND IDENTITY

Rockwell, Anne. *Career Day.* Illus. by Lizzy Rockwell. New York: HarperCollins, 2000. Unp.
❿ CIVIC IDEALS AND PRACTICES

Rotner, Shelley and Sheila Kelly, *Lots of Grandparents.* Brookfield, CT: Millbrook Press, 2003. 32 pp.
❶ CULTURE

Schertle, Alice. *Little Blue Truck Leads the Way.* Illus. by Jill McElmurry. San Diego: Harcourt, 2009. 32 pp.
❸ PEOPLE, PLACES, AND ENVIRONMENTS

Suen, Anastasia. *A Good Team: A Cooperation Story.* Illus. by Jeff Ebbeler. Edina, MN: Magic Wagon, 2008. 32 pp.
❿ CIVIC IDEALS AND PRACTICES

Willems, Mo. *Cat the Cat, Who is That?* New York: HarperCollins, 2010. Unp.
❶ CULTURE

Kindergarten

Ada, Alma Flor and F. Isabel Campoy, selectors. *Muu, Moo!: Rimas de Animales/Animal Nursery Rhymes.* English version by Rosalma Zubizarreta. Illus. by Viví Escrivá. New York: HarperCollins/Rayo, 2010. 47 pp.
❶ CULTURE

Bang, Molly. *When Sophie Gets Angry – Really, Really Angry.* New York: Blue Sky Press, 1999. Unp.
❹ INDIVIDUAL DEVELOPMENT AND IDENTITY

Becker, Bonny. *A Visitor for Bear.* Illus. by Kady MacDonald Denton. Somerville, MA: Candlewick Press, 2008. 32 pp.
❹ INDIVIDUAL DEVELOPMENT AND IDENTITY

Bloom, Suzanne. *What About Bear?* Honesdale, PA: Boyds Mills Press, 2010. 32 pp.
❿ CIVIC IDEALS AND PRACTICES

Cadena, Beth. *Supersister.* Illus. by Frank W. Dormer. New York: Clarion, 2009. 32 pp.
❹ INDIVIDUAL DEVELOPMENT AND IDENTITY

Chaconas, Dori. *Cork and Fuzz: Finders Keepers.* Illus. by Lisa McCue. New York: Viking, 2009. 32 pp.
❿ CIVIC IDEALS AND PRACTICES

Crews, Donald. *Shortcut.* New York: HarperCollins, Greenwillow, 1992. Unp.
❹ INDIVIDUAL DEVELOPMENT AND IDENTITY

Heiligman, Deborah. *Cool Dog, School Dog.* Illus. by Tim Bowers. New York: Marshall Cavendish Children's Books, 2009. 32 pp.
❺ INDIVIDUALS, GROUPS, AND INSTITUTIONS

Henkes, Kevin. *My Garden.* New York: HarperCollins, Greenwillow, 2010. 32 pp.
❸ PEOPLE, PLACES, AND ENVIRONMENTS

Henson, Heather. *That Book Woman.* Illus. by David Small. New York: Atheneum, 2008. 40 pp.
❷ TIME, CONTINUITY, AND CHANGE

Hubbell, Patricia. *Teacher: Sharing, Helping, Caring.* Illus. by Nancy Speir. New York: Marshall Cavendish Children, 2009. 32 pp.
❿ CIVIC IDEALS AND PRACTICES

Klise, Kate. *Imagine Harry.* Illus. by M. Sarah Klise. San Diego: Harcourt, 2007. Unp.
❹ INDIVIDUAL DEVELOPMENT AND IDENTITY

Long, Loren. *Otis.* New York: Penguin, Philomel, 2009. 32 pp.
❽ SCIENCE, TECHNOLOGY, AND SOCIETY

Lord, Cynthia. *Hot Rod Hamster.* Illus. by Derek Anderson. New York: Scholastic, 2010. 32 pp.
❽ SCIENCE, TECHNOLOGY, AND SOCIETY

McMullan, Kate. *I'm Big.* Illus. by Jim McMullan. New York: HarperCollins, 2010. 32 pp.
❹ INDIVIDUAL DEVELOPMENT AND IDENTITY

Peet, Mal & Elspeth Graham. *Cloud Tea Monkeys.* Illus. by Juan Wijngaard. Somerville, MA: Candlewick Press, 2010. 56 pp.
❸ PEOPLE, PLACES, AND ENVIRONMENTS

Rosenberry, Vera. *Vera Rides a Bike.* New York: Holt, 2004. Unp.
❹ INDIVIDUAL DEVELOPMENT AND IDENTITY

Sharp, N.L. *Effie's Image.* Illus. by Dorothia Rohner. Fremont, NE: Prairieland Press, 2004. Unp.
❹ INDIVIDUAL DEVELOPMENT AND IDENTITY

Urbanovic, Jackie. *Duck and Cover*. New York: HarperCollins, 2009. 32 pp.
❹ INDIVIDUAL DEVELOPMENT AND IDENTITY

Yolen, Jane. *Owl Moon*. Illus. by John Schoenherr. New York: Penguin, Philomel, 1987. Unp.
❸ PEOPLE, PLACES, AND ENVIRONMENTS

First Grade

Barnwell, Ysaye M. *We Are One*. Illus. by Brian Pinkney. Orlando: Harcourt, 2008. 32 pp.
❾ GLOBAL CONNECTIONS

Bottner, Barbara. *Miss Brooks Loves Books! (and I Don't)*. Illus. by Michael Emberley. New York: Knopf, 2010. 32 pp.
❹ INDIVIDUAL DEVELOPMENT AND IDENTITY

Caseley, Judith. *On the Town: A Community Adventure*. New York: HarperCollins, Greenwillow, 2002. Unp.
❻ POWER, AUTHORITY, AND GOVERNANCE

Cooper, Elisha. *Farm*. New York: Orchard Books, 2010. 32 pp.
❸ PEOPLE, PLACES, AND ENVIRONMENTS

Doner, Kim. *On a Road in Africa*. Berkeley, CA: Tricycle Press, 2008. 48 pp.
❸ PEOPLE, PLACES, AND ENVIRONMENTS

Gerdner, Linda and Sarah Langford. *Grandfather's Story Cloth*. Illus. by Stuart Loughridge. Walnut Creek, CA: Shen's Books, 2008. 32 pp.
❷ TIME, CONTINUITY, AND CHANGE

Hoberman, Mary Ann. *You Read to Me, I'll Read to You: Very Short Fairy Tales to Read Together (in which wolves are tamed, trolls are transformed, and peas are triumphant.)* Illus. by Michael Emberley. New York: Little, Brown/Megan Tingley, 2004. 32 pp.
❹ INDIVIDUAL DEVELOPMENT AND IDENTITY

Jenkins, Steve. *Never Smile at a Monkey: and 17 Other Important Things to Remember*. Boston: Houghton Mifflin Books for Children, 2009. Unp.
❸ PEOPLE, PLACES, AND ENVIRONMENTS

Jules, Jacqueline. *Duck for Turkey Day*. Illus. by Kathryn Mitter. Morton Grove, IL: Albert Whitman & Co., 2009. Unp.
❶ CULTURE

Krull, Kathleen. *Supermarket*. Illus. by Melanie Hope Greenberg. New York: Holiday House, 2001. Unp.
❼ PRODUCTION, CONSUMPTION, AND DISTRIBUTION

O'Neill, Alexis. *The Recess Queen*. Illus. by Laura Huliska-Beith. New York: Scholastic, 2002. Unp.
❻ POWER, AUTHORITY, AND GOVERNANCE

Peete, Holly Robinson and Ryan Elizabeth Peete with Denene Millner. *My Brother Charlie*. Pictures by Shane W. Evans. New York: Scholastic Press, 2010. 36 pp.
❹ INDIVIDUAL DEVELOPMENT AND IDENTITY

Reynolds, Aaron. *Metal Man*. Illus. by Paul Hoppe. Watertown, MA: Charlesbridge, 2008. 32 pp.
❶ CULTURE

Scieszka, Jon. *Truckery Rhymes*. Illus. by David Shannon, Loren Long, David Gordon and others. New York: Simon & Schuster, 2009. 57 pp.
❽ SCIENCE, TECHNOLOGY, AND SOCIETY

Sheth, Kashmira. *Monsoon Afternoon*. Illus. by Yoshiko Jaeggi. Atlanta, GA: Peachtree Publishers, 2008. 32 pp.
❸ PEOPLE, PLACES, AND ENVIRONMENTS

Sidman, Joyce. *Red Sings from Treetops: a Year in Colors*. Illus. by Pamela Zagarenski. Boston: Houghton Mifflin Books for Children, 2009. Unp.
❸ PEOPLE, PLACES, AND ENVIRONMENTS

Simon, Norma. *All Kinds of Children*. Illus. by Diane Paterson. Morton Grove, IL: Albert Whitman & Co, 1999. 32 pp.
❾ GLOBAL CONNECTIONS

Solheim, James. *Born Yesterday: The Diary of a Young Journalist*. Illus. by Simon James. New York: Penguin, Philomel, 2010. unp.
❹ INDIVIDUAL DEVELOPMENT AND IDENTITY

Wolff, Ashley. *I Call My Grandma Nana*. Berkeley, CA: Tricycle Press, 2009. 30 pp.
❶ CULTURE

Wolff, Ashley. *I Call My Grandpa Papa*. Berkeley, CA: Tricycle Press, 2009. 30 pp.
❶ CULTURE

Blue, Rose and Corinne J. Naden. *Ron's Big Mission.* Illus. by Don Tate. New York: Penguin, Dutton Children's Books, 2009. 32 pp.
❷ TIME, CONTINUITY, AND CHANGE

Brown, Don. *A Wizard from the Start: the Incredible Boyhood and Amazing Inventions of Thomas Edison.* Boston: Houghton Mifflin Books for Children Books for Children, 2010. Unp.
❽ SCIENCE, TECHNOLOGY, AND SOCIETY

Chocolate, Debbi. *El Barrio.* Illus. by David Diaz. New York: Henry Holt Books for Young Readers, 2009. 32 pp.
❶ CULTURE

Cole, Joanna. *The Magic School Bus & The Climate Challenge.* Illus. by Bruce Degen. New York: Scholastic, 2010. 40 pp.
❸ PEOPLE, PLACES, AND ENVIRONMENTS

Crandell, Rachel. *Hands of the Rain Forest: The Embera People of Panama.* New York: Henry Holt Books for Young Readers, 2009. 32 pp.
❶ CULTURE

George, Jean Craighead. *The Wolves Are Back.* Illus. by Wendell Minor. New York: Penguin, Dutton Children's Books, 2008. 32 pp.
❸ PEOPLE, PLACES, AND ENVIRONMENTS

Hollyer, Beatrice. *Our World of Water: Children and Water around the World.* New York: Henry Holt Books for Young Readers, 2009. 48 pp.
❸ PEOPLE, PLACES, AND ENVIRONMENTS

Kerley, Barbara. *What to do about Alice?: How Alice Roosevelt Broke the Rules, Charmed the World, and Drove Her Father Teddy Crazy!* Illus. by Edwin Fotheringham. New York: Scholastic, 2008. 48 pp.
❷ TIME, CONTINUITY, AND CHANGE

Khan, Rukhsana. *Big Red Lollipop.* Illus. by Sophie Blackall. New York: Viking, 2010. 32 pp.
❶ CULTURE

Kimmelman, Leslie. *Mind Your Manners, Alice Roosevelt!* Illus. by Adam Gustavson. Atlanta, GA: Peachtree Publishers, 2009. 32 pp.
❷ TIME, CONTINUITY, AND CHANGE

Look, Lenore. *Alvin Ho: Allergic to Girls, School and Other Scary Things.* Illus. by LeUyen Pham. New York: Random House Children's Books, Schwartz & Wade, 2008. 172 pp.
❹ INDIVIDUAL DEVELOPMENT AND IDENTITY

Ludwig, Trudy. *Trouble Talk.* Illus. by Mikela Prevost. Foreword by Charisse L. Nixon. Berkeley, CA: Tricycle Press, 2008. 32 pp.
❺ INDIVIDUALS, GROUPS, AND INSTITUTIONS

Lyon, George Ella and Stephanie Anderson. *You and Me and Home Sweet Home.* New York: Atheneum/Richard Jackson Books, 2009. 48 pp.
❺ INDIVIDUALS, GROUPS, AND INSTITUTIONS

McPhail, David. *No!* New York: Roaring Brook Press, 2009. 48 pp.
❻ POWER, AUTHORITY, AND GOVERNANCE

Say, Allan. *Erika-San.* Boston: Houghton Mifflin Harcourt, 2009. 32 pp.
❶ CULTURE

Sheth, Kashmira. *My Dadima Wears a Sari.* Illus. by Yoshiko Jaeggi. Atlanta, GA: Peachtree Publishers, 2007. 32 pp.
❶ CULTURE

Smith, Penny and Zahavit Shalev. *A School Like Mine: A Unique Celebration of Schools around the World.* New York: DK Publishing and UNICEF, 2007. 80 pp.
❾ GLOBAL CONNECTIONS

Williams, Karen Lynn and Khadra Mohammed. *My Name is Sangoel.* Illus. by Catherine Stock. Grand Rapids, MI: Eerdmans Books for Young Readers, 2009. 32 pp.
❶ CULTURE

Winter, Jeanette. *Wangari's Tree of Peace: A True Story from Africa.* San Diego: Harcourt Children's Books, 2008. 32 pp.
❸ PEOPLE, PLACES, AND ENVIRONMENTS

Winter, Jonah. *You Never Heard of Sandy Koufax?* Illus. by Andre Carrilho. New York: Random House Children's Books, Schwartz & Wade, 2009. 40 pp.
❺ INDIVIDUALS, GROUPS, AND INSTITUTIONS

Ajmera, Maya, Magda Nakassis, and Cynthia Pon. *Faith*. Watertown, MA: Charlesbridge Publishing, 2009. 48 pp.
❾ GLOBAL CONNECTIONS

Campbell, Bebe Moore. *I Get So Hungry*. Illus. by Amy Bates. New York: Penguin, G. P. Putnam, 2008. 32 pp.
❹ INDIVIDUAL DEVELOPMENT AND IDENTITY

Davies, Jacqueline. *Tricking the Tallyman: The Great Census Shananigans of 1790*. Illus. by S.D. Schindler. New York: Alfred A. Knopf Books for Young Readers, 2009. 40 pp.
❿ CIVIC IDEALS AND PRACTICES

Grigsby, Susan. *In the Garden with Dr. Carver*. Pictures by Nicole Tadgell. Chicago: Albert Whitman, 2010. 32 pp.
❽ SCIENCE, TECHNOLOGY, AND SOCIETY

Grimes, Nikki. *Barack Obama: Son of Promise, Child of Hope*. Illus. by Bryan Collier. New York: Simon & Schuster Books for Young Readers, 2008. 48 pp.
❷ TIME, CONTINUITY, AND CHANGE

Harrington, Janice. *Going North*. Pictures by Jerome Lagarrigue. New York: Farrar, Straus & Giroux, 2004. 40 pp.
❷ TIME, CONTINUITY, AND CHANGE

Hill, Laban Carrick. *Dave the Potter: Artist, Poet, Slave*. Illus. by Bryan Collier. New York: Little, Brown & Co., 2010. 40 pp.
❹ INDIVIDUAL DEVELOPMENT AND IDENTITY

Hopkinson, Deborah. *Keep On! The Story of Matthew Henson, Co-Discoverer of the North Pole*. Illus. by Stephen Alcorn. Atlanta, GA: Peachtree Publishers, 2009. 36 pp.
❷ TIME, CONTINUITY, AND CHANGE

Hopkinson, Deborah. *Michelle*. Illus. by A.G. Ford. New York: HarperCollins Children's Books, 2009. 32 pp.
❷ TIME, CONTINUITY, AND CHANGE

Jackson, Ellen. *The Cupcake Thief*. Illus. by Blanche Sims. New York: Kane Press, 2007. 32 pp.
❻ POWER, AUTHORITY, AND GOVERNANCE

Kajikawa, Kimiko. *Tsunami!* Illus. by Ed Young. New York: Penguin, Philomel Books, 2009. 32 pp.
❸ PEOPLE, PLACES, AND ENVIRONMENTS

Kerley, Barbara. *A Little Peace*. With a Note by Richard H. Solomon. Illus. by various photographers. Washington, DC: National Geographic Society, 2007. 32 pp.
❺ INDIVIDUALS, GROUPS, AND INSTITUTIONS

Kerley, Barbara. *One World, One Day*. Washington, DC: National Geographic Children's Books, 2009. 48 pp.
❾ GLOBAL CONNECTIONS

Lane, Kimberly. *Come Look with Me: Latin American Art*. Watertown, MA: Charlesbridge, 2007. 32 pp.
❶ CULTURE

Moss, Marissa. *Sky High: The True Story of Maggie Gee*. Illus. by Carl Angel. Berkeley, CA: Tricycle Press, 2009. 32 pp.
❷ TIME, CONTINUITY, AND CHANGE

Proimos, James. *Paulie Pastrami Achieves World Peace*. New York: Little, Brown Books for Young Readers, 2009. 40 pp.
❹ INDIVIDUAL DEVELOPMENT AND IDENTITY

Ritchie, Scot. *Follow That Map! A First Book of Mapping Skills*. Toronto, Canada: Kids Can Press, 2009. 32 pp.
❸ PEOPLE, PLACES, AND ENVIRONMENTS

Shulevitz, Uri. *How I Learned Geography*. New York: Farrar, Straus & Giroux Books for Young Readers, 2008. 32 pp.
❸ PEOPLE, PLACES, AND ENVIRONMENTS

Whelan, Gloria. *Waiting for the Owl's Call*. Illus. by Pascal Milelli. Chelsea, MI: Sleeping Bear Press, 2009. 32 pp.
❶ CULTURE

Winter, Jeanette. *Nasreen's Secret School: A True Story from Afghanistan*. New York: Beach Lane Books, 2009. 40 pp.
❶ CULTURE

Alalou, Elizabeth and Ali Alalou. *The Butter Man.* Illus. by Julie Klear Essakalli. Watertown, MA: Charlesbridge, 2008. 32 pp.
❶ CULTURE

Buckley, Carol. *Tarra & Bella: the Elephant and Dog Who Became Best Friends.* New York: Penguin, Putnam, 2009. Unp.
❹ INDIVIDUAL DEVELOPMENT AND IDENTITY

Clement, Andrew. *Extra Credit.* Illus. by Mark Elliot. New York: Atheneum, 2009. 183 pp.
❾ GLOBAL CONNECTIONS

Cummins, Julie. *Women Daredevils: Thrills, Chills, and Frills.* Illus. by Cheryl Harness. New York: Penguin, Dutton's Children's Books, 2008. 48 pp.
❷ TIME, CONTINUITY, AND CHANGE

Dillon, Leo and Diane. *Jazz on a Saturday Night.* New York: Blue Sky Press, 2007. 40 pp.
❶ CULTURE

Hall, Alvin. *Show Me the Money: How to Make Cents of Economics.* New York: DK Publishing, 2008. 96 pp.
❼ PRODUCTION, CONSUMPTION, AND DISTRIBUTION

Kooser, Ted. *Bag in the Wind.* Illus. by Barry Root. Somerville, MA: Candlewick Press, 2010. 32 pp.
❸ PEOPLE, PLACES, AND ENVIRONMENTS

Larson, Kirby and Mary Nethery. *Two Bobbies: A True Story of Hurricane Katrina, Friendship, and Survival.* Illus. by Jean Cassels. New York: Walker Books for Young Children, 2008. 32 pp.
❿ CIVIC IDEALS AND PRACTICES

Mortenson, Greg and Susan L. Roth. *Listen to the Wind: The Story of Dr. Greg and Three Cups of Tea.* Illus. by Susan L. Roth. New York: Penguin, Dial Books for Young Readers, 2009. 32 pp.
❾ GLOBAL CONNECTIONS

Nivola, Claire A. *Planting the Trees of Kenya: The Story of Wangari Maathai.* New York: Farrar, Straus & Giroux Books for Young Readers, 2008. 32 pp.
❸ PEOPLE, PLACES, AND ENVIRONMENTS

O'Connor, Barbara. *How to Steal a Dog.* New York: Farrar, Straus and Giroux, Frances Foster Books, 2007. 170 pp.
❹ INDIVIDUAL DEVELOPMENT AND IDENTITY

Rabin, Staton. *Mr. Lincoln's Boys: Being the Mostly True Adventures of Abraham Lincoln's Trouble-Making Sons, Tad and Willie.* Illus. by Bagram Ibatoulline. New York: Viking Children's Books, 2008. 36 pp.
❷ TIME, CONTINUITY, AND CHANGE

Ramsey, Calvin Alexander, with Gwen Strauss. *Ruth and the Green Book.* Illus. by Floyd Cooper. Minneapolis, MN: Lerner, Carolrhoda Books, 2010. 32 pp.
❷ TIME, CONTINUITY, AND CHANGE

Rappaport, Doreen. *Lady Liberty: A Biography.* Illus. by Matt Tavares. Somerville, MA: Candlewick Press, 2008. 40 pp.
❷ TIME, CONTINUITY, AND CHANGE

Rumford, James. *Silent Music: A Story of Baghdad.* New York: Roaring Brook Press, 2008. 32 pp.
❶ CULTURE

Sanders, Nancy I. *D is for Drinking Gourd: An African American Alphabet.* Illus. by E.B. Lewis. Chelsea, MI: Sleeping Bear Press, 2007. 40 pp.
❶ CULTURE

Skeers, Linda. *The Impossible Patriotism Project.* Illus. by Ard Hoyt. New York: Penguin, Dial Books for Young Readers, 2007. 32 pp.
❿ CIVIC IDEALS AND PRACTICES

Van Wyk, Chris, abridged by. *Nelson Mandela: Long Walk to Freedom.* Illus. by Paddy Bouma. New York: Roaring Brook Press, 2009. 64 pp.
❷ TIME, CONTINUITY, AND CHANGE

Williams, Karen Lynn and Khadra Mohammed. *Four Feet, Two Sandals.* Illus. by Doug Chayka. Grand Rapids, MI: Eerdmans Books for Young Readers, 2007. 32 pp.
❹ INDIVIDUAL DEVELOPMENT AND IDENTITY

Winter, Jonah. *Steel Town.* Illus. by Terry Widener. New York: Atheneum, 2008. 40 pp.
❽ SCIENCE, TECHNOLOGY, AND SOCIETY

Fifth Grade

Anderson, Lauri Halse. *Independent Dames: What You Never Knew about the Women and Girls of the American Revolution*. Illus. by Matt Faulkner. New York: Simon & Schuster Books for Young Readers, 2008. 40 pp.
❷ TIME, CONTINUITY, AND CHANGE

Deedy, Carmen Agra in collaboration with Wilson Kimeli Naiyomah. *14 Cows for America*. Illus. by Thomas Gonzalez. Atlanta, GA: Peachtree Publishers, 2009. 36 pp.
❶ CULTURE

Dicks, Lynn et al. *Earth Matters: an Encyclopedia of Ecology*. New York: DK Publishing, 2008. 96 pp.
❸ PEOPLE, PLACES, AND ENVIRONMENTS

Fletcher, Susan. *Dadblamed Union Army Cow*. Illus. by Kimberly Bulcken Root. Somerville, MA: Candlewick Press, 2007. 32 pp.
❹ INDIVIDUAL DEVELOPMENT AND IDENTITY

Freedman, Russell. *Freedom Walkers: The Story of the Montgomery Bus Boycott*. New York: Holiday House, 2006. 114 pp.
❷ TIME, CONTINUITY, AND CHANGE

Harness, Cheryl. *The Groundbreaking, Chance-Taking Life of George Washington Carver and Science and Invention in America*. Washington, DC: National Geographic Children's Books, 2008. 143 pp.
❽ SCIENCE, TECHNOLOGY, AND SOCIETY

Hopkins, Lee Bennett, selector. *America at War: Poems*. Illus. by Stephen Alcorn. New York: Simon & Schuster, Margaret K. McElderry Books, 2008. 84 pp.
❷ TIME, CONTINUITY, AND CHANGE

Hopkinson, Deborah. *Up Before Daybreak: Cotton and People In America*. New York: Scholastic, 2006. 120 pp.
❼ PRODUCTION, CONSUMPTION, AND DISTRIBUTION

Mackall, Dandi Daley. *Rudy Rides the Rails: A Depression Era Story*. Illus. by Chris Ellison. Chelsea, MI: Sleeping Bear Press, 2007. 40 pp.
❷ TIME, CONTINUITY, AND CHANGE

Michelson, Richard. *As Good As Anybody: Martin Luther King Jr. and Abraham Joshua Heschel's Amazing March toward Freedom*. Illus. by Raul Colon. New York: Alfred A. Knopf/Random House Children's Books, 2008. 40 pp.
❷ TIME, CONTINUITY, AND CHANGE

National Children's Book and Literacy Alliance. *Our White House, Looking In, Looking Out*. Somerville, MA: Candlewick Press, 2008. 256 pp.
❷ TIME, CONTINUITY, AND CHANGE

O'Brien, Tony and Mike Sullivan. *Afghan Dreams: Young Voices of Afghanistan*. Photos by Tony O'Brien. New York: Bloomsbury USA Children's Books, 2008. 69 pp.
❶ CULTURE

Paulsen, Gary. *Lawn Boy*. New York: Random House Children's Books, 2007. 88 pp.
❼ PRODUCTION, CONSUMPTION, AND DISTRIBUTION

Peck, Richard. *On the Wings of Heroes*. New York: Penguin, Dial Books for Young Readers, 2007. 148 pp.
❷ TIME, CONTINUITY, AND CHANGE

Pinkney, Andrea Davis. *Boycott Blues: How Rosa Parks Inspired a Nation*. Illus. by Brian Pinkney. New York: HarperCollins, Greenwillow, 2008. 40 pp.
❷ TIME, CONTINUITY, AND CHANGE

Schrock, Jan West. *Give a Goat*. Illus. by Aileen Darragh. Gardiner, ME: Tilbury House, 2008. 32 pp.
❾ GLOBAL CONNECTIONS

Scillian, Devin. *Pappy's Handkerchief*. Illus. by Chris Ellison. Chelsea, MI: Sleeping Bear Press, 2007. 40 pp.
❸ PEOPLE, PLACES, AND ENVIRONMENTS

Silvey, Anita. *I'll Pass for Your Comrade: Women Soldiers in the Civil War*. New York: Clarion Books, 2008. 112 pp.
❷ TIME, CONTINUITY, AND CHANGE

Winters, Kay. *Colonial Voices: Hear Them Speak*. Illus. by Larry Day. New York: Penguin, Dutton Children's Books, 2008. 32 pp.
❷ TIME, CONTINUITY, AND CHANGE

Wise, Bill. *Louis Sockalexis: Native American Baseball Pioneer*. Illus. by Bill Farnsworth. New York: Lee & Low, 2009. 31 pp.
❷ TIME, CONTINUITY, AND CHANGE

Contributors

Editors

PEGGY ALTOFF is a retired district social studies coordinator and independent consultant. She served as President of National Council for the Social Studies (NCSS) in 2006-2007.

SYD GOLSTON is a curriculum writer and school administrator. She served as President of National Council for the Social Studies in 2009-2010.

Other Authors

CHARLEE ARCHULETA has served on the editorial board of the NCSS journal for elementary educators, *Social Studies and the Young Learner*. She teaches 4tth grade in District 11, Colorado Springs, CO.

LINDA B. BENNETT is in the Provost Office at the University of Missouri. She has been an elementary social studies educator for more than thirty years, and served as the editor of *Social Studies and the Young Learner* from 2006-2010.

NANCY P. GALLAVAN is a professor of teacher education in the Department of Teaching and Learning, MAT Program, at the University of Central Arkansas.

LEANNA GUILLORY has taught third grade at Shepard Elementary in Columbia, Missouri for 5 years. She is currently serving as a mentor teacher through the Fellows Program at the University of Missouri, Columbia.

ELIZABETH R. HINDE is an associate professor of teacher education at the Mary Lou Fulton Teachers College, Arizona State University.

PATRICIA KENNEDY is a Reading Specialist in the Scottsdale, Arizona schools. She has had over 25 years of teaching experience in the early childhood grades.

BARBARA KNIGHTON is a 4th grade teacher and education consultant who lives in Michigan. She has over 20 years of teaching experience, and has written several books and articles on teaching and social studies.

MEREDITH McGOWAN is the Curator of the Jane Pope Geske Heritage Room of Nebraska Authors, Lincoln City Libraries. She has worked for many years with young people, sharing her interest in curricular connections, especially with social studies.

KATHY J. MOORE is director of the Child Study Center and an instructor in the Department of Early Childhood/Special Education at the University of Central Arkansas.

JOAN BRODSKY SCHUR is an education consultant, curriculum developer and teacher trainer. She serves as Social Studies Consultant to the City and Country School, and is an Adjunct Instructor at the Bank Street College of Education, both in New York City.

CAROL CARNEY WARREN has had over 25 years of teaching experience in the elementary grades, and has served as the social studies specialist for the Arizona Department of Education.

NCSS AND THE ELEMENTARY TEACHER

National Council for the Social Studies (NCSS) is the nation's leading association of social studies educators at all K-12 grade levels.

NCSS is strongly committed to excellent instruction in social studies in elementary schools. NCSS publications offer elementary teachers lesson plans and class activities in social studies, and focus regularly on children's literature that is of special value for teaching social studies in the elementary grades. Every year, in cooperation with the Children's Book Council, NCSS publishes an annual list of Notable Social Studies Trade Books for Young People, which identifies and annotates outstanding children's books published the previous year. All NCSS individual and institutional members receive the issue of the NCSS journal, *Social Education*, in which this list is published.

The NCSS periodical, *Social Studies and the Young Learner*, is a benefit of NCSS membership for K-6 elementary educators. This colorful, peer-reviewed journal features teaching ideas, lesson plans, and handouts that enhance social studies teaching in K-6 classrooms.

A special category of NCSS membership is "comprehensive membership." NCSS comprehensive members automatically receive books in the NCSS Bulletin series (such as this book) free of charge.

Information about membership in NCSS is available at www.socialstudies.org/membership

In 2010, NCSS developed and published the *National Curriculum Standards for Social Studies: A Framework for Teaching, Learning, and Assessment*, which are used in this book. These national standards establish learning expectations for the elementary, middle, and high school levels. The standards place a special emphasis on the purposes of social studies, questions for exploration, expectations for the development of the knowledge and abilities of students, and products through which learners demonstrate understanding. Further information about the standards is available at www.socialstudies.org/standards

National Council for the Social Studies
8555 Sixteenth Street • Suite 500 • Silver Spring, Maryland 20910

www.**socialstudies**.org